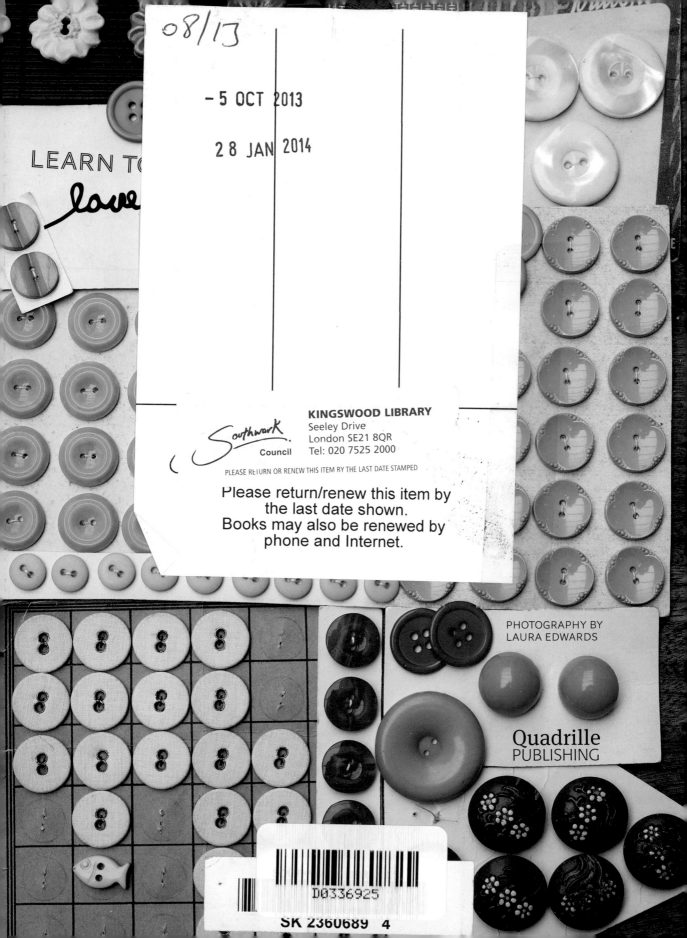

LEARN TO
love

PHOTOGRAPHY BY
LAURA EDWARDS

Quadrille
PUBLISHING

4 Introduction
6 Basic knitting kit
8 Understanding yarns, patterns and abbreviations
10 Basic knitting techniques

LEARN TO KNIT PROJECTS
32 Striped scarf and mittens with giant pompoms
36 Shopper with dropped stitch detail
40 Wristwarmers with contrast rib
44 His or hers bobble hats
48 Hand puff and collar with embroidery
52 Simple round neck sweater with raglan sleeves
58 Cropped cardigan with cabled sleeves
64 Lace collar with tie fastening
70 Lace top with bow
76 Random striped sweater

LOVE TO KNIT PROJECTS
82 College-style cardigan with patch pocket
88 Shawl collar cardigan with floral embroidery
96 Fair Isle band sweater with short sleeves
102 Textured cardigan with ribbed waist
108 Fair Isle rib tanktop
114 Cabled tam and snood
118 Polka-dot socks
122 Cabled cardigan with short sleeves
126 Tartan sweater with three-quarter length sleeves
136 Tweed cape

141 Yarn information
144 Acknowledgements

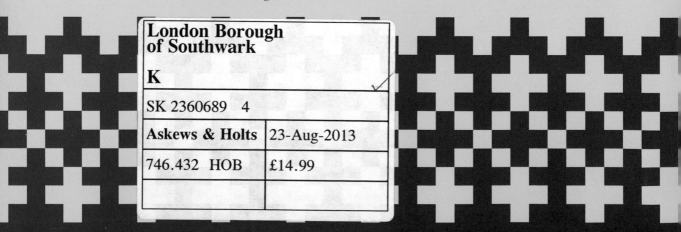

WHEN I WAS LEARNING TO KNIT,

I found the hardest part was getting used to how the yarn and needles felt in my hands and how to manipulate them with my fingers. I remember my hands feeling very rigid and awkward at first, but this feeling quickly passed with just a little persistence, practice and a few inevitable dropped stitches. Once you have learnt the basic knit stitch, and really got the hang of it, I believe anything is possible. Every other knitted stitch is just a variation of this one technique and, once you are familiar with the basics, you will be well on your way to mastering any pattern you put your mind to.

The **LEARN TO KNIT** projects in the first section of this book include some very basic and straightforward patterns, so starting with these will enable you to become familiar with the craft and the simpler knit stitches. The patterns then build in difficulty, introducing techniques in different projects, giving you the chance to learn and practice new skills. Some of the **LOVE TO KNIT** projects towards the end of this book may look daunting, but everything is perfectly achievable. Certain projects are simply more time consuming than others and may require more concentration. Just remember, do not panic if you go wrong or drop a stitch. The beauty of knitting is that stitches can easily be unravelled and reknitted.

My career in knitwear really launched for me when I graduated from Winchester School of Art in 2009 and went on to win the Gold Award in the Knitted Textile Awards, which was showcased at the Knitting and Stitching Show at Alexandra Palace. This was an amazing opportunity for me. I met designers, including Debbie Bliss, who I've since had the pleasure of working with on a freelance basis. Before all of this though, a long time ago, I learnt to knit at quite a young age. I was taught by my mother, who really encouraged myself and my two brothers to be creative in all ways; I really wouldn't be writing this book now if it wasn't for all her support. I grew up with colour, art and textiles around me, so now I really can't imagine doing anything else. I'm just so grateful to be able to spend my time doing something that I love and call it 'work'.

While at university, I learnt to machine knit; however, for me, there is no comparison between hand knitting and machine knitting. Hand knitting is charming and has personality, plus the labour involved makes it utterly priceless. Whether you wear it yourself or give it as an incredibly generous gift, a hand knit will be loved and worn until it is falling apart and threadbare. You simply cannot create something so special using a machine. The possibilities with hand knitting are endless – you can dream up practically anything and make it yourself. Within this book, I have produced a collection of garments and accessories that I loved designing and making, and each of which I want to wear myself. I really hope that you too enjoy making these projects, whether you are a beginner or have been knitting for years, and I hope that you feel inspired to continue knitting and exploring other patterns and possibilities.

IN YOUR BASIC KNITTING TOOL KIT YOU WILL NEED

KNITTING NEEDLES Knitting needles come in a variety of lengths and thicknesses, depending on the yarn you are knitting with and how many stitches you want to hold on your needle. You will find that when you knit with really thick yarn you will need thicker needles, and the finer the yarn you are using the thinner the needles you will need to use. When you buy yarn, the label always has a suggested needle size on it, but you can always play around with if you want a tighter or looser stitch. You can also get circular needles for knitting in the round. Basically, these are two shorter needles connected by a long nylon wire. You can use circular needles for knitting in rows as well as working in the round, just make sure at the end of each row you swap the needles over in your hands and knit back the way you've just come, rather than continue to knit round and round.

STITCH HOLDERS You will need a few stitch holders when knitting garments. They are used for holding stitches securely that are currently not being worked, for example, around a neckline while you continue with a different section of knitting. Then stitches are then later returned to the needles from the stitch holder once you are ready to work with those stitches again. Safety pins are a good alternative for holding a small number of stitches.

CABLE NEEDLES Cable needles are small open-ended needles used for holding just a few stitches at a time and are used when you make the twist in a cable.

DARNING NEEDLE Make sure that you have a few needles with a big enough eye to fit yarn through for stitching up knitted garments. It's preferable not to use needles that are too fine as sometimes you find yourself stitching through the knitted yarn and splitting it. You could use a bodkin, which is similar to a needle but is very thick with a big eye so it's perfect for stitching up chunkier knitted garments.

PINS AND SAFETY PINS These are always useful for pinning seams together before you stitch them, so you know you're sewing evenly.

TAPE MEASURE A tape measure is essential for checking that your tension is correct. Also, you may find that some patterns use measurements instead of row numbers.

PEN AND PAPER For marking off where you are in your pattern and making other notes.

SCISSORS For snipping yarn.

ROW COUNTERS These are tiny cylinders with rotating numbers that you can slip on one of your knitting needles. Each time you complete a row or round, change the number so you know where you are in your knitting pattern at all times.

NEEDLE GAUGE If you have a collection of vintage knitting needles, which can be picked up from charity shops or car boot sales, a gauge is really useful. As the old imperial sizing system isn't the same as new metric one, this will confirm the size of a needle.

CROCHET HOOK I love to combine knitting with crochet by adding crocheted buttons or edges to a garment. However, if you don't want to add crochet to your knits, a crochet hook is essential to a knitter's kit as it is the perfect tool for picking up dropped stitches.

CHOOSING YARNS

Select your yarns with care. There are so many amazing hand-knit yarns to choose from, available in a range of different thicknesses and a multitude of colours. I wholeheartedly recommend investing in good quality yarn as it's more enjoyable to work with and your final knitted piece will look and feel so much nicer to wear and use. Many of the projects in this book are knitted with some really stunning yarn... however, some of these yarns are quite expensive. If you don't feel like splashing out on the specific recommended yarn, another yarn of the same thickness may be substituted.

For example, if I recommended using a double-knitting weight yarn you can substitute this for another DK yarn. Just make sure that you work a tension swatch and match the recommended tension given at the beginning of the pattern.

Whatever you choose, the yarn label or ball band will provide information on how to use and care for the yarn. As well as a recommended needle size and tension, the label will also give the weight and length of the yarn so you can get a rough idea of how far it will go. With the majority of hand-knitted garments, it is best to hand wash gently and leave to dry as flat as possible so the garment does not stretch with the weight of the water as it dries. When buying more than one ball of a specific yarn, check they all have the same dye lot number. Although the balls of yarn may look the same, there can be subtle colour differences between batches, which may show when knitted. While knitting a project, keep a note of the dye lot number should you need to buy more yarn.

READING PATTERNS

A pattern works through all elements of the project, giving the necessary instructions for every part. Beginning with the size of needles, shade of yarn and number of stitches cast on, the pattern then continues to outline, row by row, the stitch pattern to follow and indicates when any shaping or other details, such as buttonholes, must be worked. It takes a while to become familiar with the language of knitting patterns, so opposite is a handy list of the most commonly used abbreviations.

When following any pattern, be aware of the different usage of round brackets ( ) and square brackets [ ]. Round brackets indicate the different measurements or stitches given for multiple sizes. If you choose to knit the medium size of the Simple Round Neck Sweater on page 53, for example, then you must follow the third size given in the pattern. So where the instructions state: Using 3mm needles, cast on 111 (115: 121: 127: 133) sts to knit the medium size you must cast on 121 stitches, the third number listed. The first size is always shown outside the round brackets and the remaining sizes within them. Likewise, brackets are used for specific measurements within a pattern of different sizes. So where the instructions state: Cont to work in stocking stitch until Back measures 37.5 (37.5: 38.5: 38.5: 38.5)cm to knit the medium size, again, you must follow the third measurement listed which is 38.5cm. Some knitting patterns also use square brackets, which have nothing to do with sizing but relate to repeating instructions.

TIPS FOR BEGINNERS

PRACTICE HOLDING THE YARN – Wrap the working end of the yarn (the one attached to the ball) once around the index finger of your right hand. Everyone has their own way of holding the yarn, but while you are learning this is the easiest way to keep the yarn in the correct place. It also helps to produce an even tension when knitting.

WORK A TENSION SWATCH – It's so important to get into the habit of knitting a tension swatch. No matter how tempting it is to dive in and begin the pattern, you need to know that you are working to the correct tension. If your tension isn't right, you may end up with a garment that doesn't fit. Use the tension swatch for practising your basic stitches, as well as casting on and off. Afterwards, put them to use by stitching lots together to make a throw.

READ THE PATTERN – Before you start knitting, take the time to read through all the instructions so you know what to expect. As you work through the pattern, either tick off where you are or keep a row counter handy so you don't get lost or forget which part you've already knitted.

COUNT YOUR STITCHES – Counting your stitches at the end of each row means you'll know immediately when something has gone wrong and can correct the mistake.

START SMALL – As a beginner knitter, start with a small, simple project before increasing the level of difficulty. It's tempting to be brave and try a complex pattern straight away, but things could go wrong and leave you feeling frustrated. Practice the basic knit techniques with simple projects, become confident and comfortable with these, before advancing to a more demanding pattern.

JOIN A KNITTING GROUP – Find a knitting buddy or join a group. When teaching yourself to knit, at times it can be frustrating so it's good to be surrounded by others who can answer questions and offer help. You can learn just by watching other knitters. It's also a good way to meet people, share ideas and feel inspired by what they are creating.

ENJOY YOURSELF – Knitting is a relaxing hobby, so enjoy the craft. Don't get bogged down trying to master instantly every technique and don't panic if you go wrong or drop a stitch. Have fun playing around with the endless possibilities of knitting. Think of ways to use up leftover yarn, make gifts for your friends and express your creativity.

ABBREVIATIONS

Knitting patterns use a lot of standard abbreviations for common knitting terms. Below is a list of the most widely used abbreviations and the instructions they stand for. In addition, special abbreviations may also be included at the start of a pattern, such as the directions for a specific cable stitch.

ALT	alternate
BEG	begin(ning)
CONT	continue(ing)
DEC	decrease(s)(ing)
FOLL	follow(s)(ing)
G	gram(s)
GT ST	garter stitch
INC	increase(s)(ing)
K	knit
KI-B	knit the stitch below the one on the needle
K2TOG	knit 2 stitches together
KFB	knit into front and back of next stitch
LH	left-hand
MI	make one (see page 21)
P	purl
PATT(S)	pattern(s)
PSSO	pass slipped stitch over
P2SSO	pass 2 slipped stitches over
REM	remain(s)(ing)
REP	repeat(s)(ing)
RH	right-hand
RS	right side
SKPO	slip 1, knit 1, pass slipped stitch over
SK2TOGPO	skip 1, knit 2 together, pass slipped stitch over
S2TOGKPO	slip 2 together, knit 1, pass slipped stitches over
SL	slip
SSK	slip, slip, knit these 2 stitches together
SSP	slip, slip, purl these 2 stitches together
ST(S)	stitch(es)
ST ST	stocking stitch
TBL	through back loop
TOG	together
WS	wrong side
YB	yarn back (as if to knit)
YF	yarn forward (as if to purl)
YO	yarn over (also known as yon)
YRN	yarn around needle
Y2RN	yarn round needle twice (to make 2 stitches)
[ ]	work instructions within square brackets as many times as directed

MAKING A SLIPKNOT

"The slipknot is the very first stitch you make when starting any piece of knitting. Without the slipknot you won't be able to work a single row as it acts as the anchor for all knitting, so this is the first technique you need to practice and master. Once you know how, making a slip knot really is so simple."

STEP 1 Make the yarn into a loose figure-of-eight shape, holding the tail end of the yarn in your right hand and the loop in your left hand.

STEP 2 Pass the yarn from your right hand through the loop in your left hand, ensuring that you keep hold of the tail end of yarn with your right hand and hold the new loop of yarn with your left hand.

STEP 3 Pull this new loop of yarn through the left-hand loop, keeping hold of both the yarn ends in your right hand. This forms a slipknot. Place the slipknot onto the knitting needle and pull the ends to tighten. This is the first stitch.

CASTING ON STITCHES

"Casting on is the term used for when you make the first row of stitches on your knitting needle. No matter what you are making, the pattern will always start with the instruction to cast on a certain number of stitches. There are countless different methods for casting on, but this is one of the most common and the one that I most often use."

STEP 1 With the slipknot on the left-hand needle – which counts as the first stitch – insert the tip of the right-hand needle up into the stitch from the bottom. The needles should be crossed with the left-hand needle sitting over the right-hand needle.

STEP 2 Holding the needles in your left hand, with your right hand wrap the working end of the yarn – the end attached to the ball – round the back of the right-hand needle then through the middle of both needles in an anti-clockwise motion.

STEP 3 Catching the working yarn that has just been wound round the needle, bring the tip of the right-hand needle underneath the loop on the left-hand needle and to the front of the stitch.

STEP 4 Pull the new loop further through. Insert the tip of the left-hand needle up into the loop on the right-hand needle. Slide the right-hand needle out of the loop and pull the working end of the yarn to tighten. This counts as the second stitch.

STEP 5 To make subsequent stitches, insert the right-hand needle between the last two stitches on the left-hand needle and not into the stitch. Wrap the yarn around the right-hand needle, pull the loop through and place on the left-hand needle as before.

WORKING THE KNIT STITCH

"This is the key basic stitch to learn. Most other knitting stitches are a variation on the knit stitch, so this simple four-step process is an important technique to master. In a knitting pattern, the word knit is often abbreviated to a simple 'K'. So 'k1', means 'knit one stitch' while 'k 1 row' means 'knit one row'."

STEP 1 With the full needle in your left hand and empty needle in your right, insert the tip of the right-hand needle up into the last stitch on the left-hand needle. The needles should be crossed with the left-hand needle sitting over the right-hand needle.

STEP 2 With your right hand, wrap the working end of the yarn round the back of the right-hand needle then through the middle, between the tips of both crossed needles, in an anti-clockwise motion.

STEP 3 Catching the working yarn that has just been wound round the needle, bring the tip of the right-hand needle underneath the loop on the left-hand needle. Pull the working yarn through to the front of the stitch.

STEP 4 Slide the stitch just worked from the left-hand needle, leaving the new stitch on the right-hand needle. Repeat these steps until every stitch has been transferred to the right-hand needle. Swap the needles over so the stitches are again in your left hand and continue with the next row.

WORKING THE PURL STITCH

"The next technique to learn is the purl stitch. As perfect partners, the knit and purl stitches are used in combination to create endless stitch patterns. The word purl is often abbreviated in a knitting pattern to 'P'. So 'P1' means 'purl one stitch' while 'P 1 row' means 'purl one row'."

STEP 1 With the yarn sitting at the front of the work, insert the tip of the right-hand needle up into the last stitch on the left-hand needle. The needles should be crossed with the right-hand needle sitting over the left-hand needle.

STEP 2 With your right hand, wrap the working end of the yarn through the middle, between the tips of both crossed needles, and round the back of the right-hand needle to the front in an anti-clockwise motion.

STEP 3 Catching the working yarn that has just been wound round the needle, bring the tip of the right-hand needle underneath the loop on the left-hand needle. Pull the working yarn through to the back of the stitch.

STEP 4 Slide the stitch just worked from the left-hand needle, leaving the new stitch on the right-hand needle. Repeat these steps until every stitch has been transferred to the right-hand needle. Swap the needles over so the stitches are again in your left hand and continue with the next row.

WORKING RIB STITCHES

"Rib patterns are made up of alternate columns knit and purl stitches. It creates a stretchier, more elastic piece of knitting than either stocking or garter stitch, which is why rib is often used for the waistbands and cuffs of knitted garments."

Different rib patterns are worked using varying combinations of knit and purl stitches; the instructions will specify how many of each stitch to work and in what order. Shown here is single rib, also known as k1, p1 rib or 1x1 rib. With rib, the movement of the yarn to and from the back and front of the work between stitches is most important. This movement of the yarn is never written into a pattern but it is nonetheless expected.

STEP 1 Knit the first stitch as usual. Bring the yarn towards you to the front of the work, over the top and through the middle of the needles. Purl the next stitch as usual. After working this purl stitch, the yarn will naturally be at the front of the work.

STEP 2 Take the yarn to the back of the work, passing it between the needles, ready for the next knit stitch. Repeat these steps – knit one, bring the yarn to the front, purl one, take the yarn to the back – until all the stitches in the row have been worked.

"Knit and purl stitches are the basis of all knitting and once you have learnt these two stitches you will be well on your way. By just playing around with where you place these different stitches you can produce an endless number of stitches. Here are just a few examples of what you can do."

TOP LEFT **STOCKING STITCH** – if you knit one row and then purl the next row, and then carry on alternating between knit rows and purl rows then you will create stocking stitch. This stitch has a front side – the knit side – and a reverse side – the purl side.

TOP RIGHT **GARTER STITCH** – if you knit every row then you will create garter stitch, which looks the same on both sides. You will also create the same look if you purl every row, but as most knitters take longer to work the

purl stitch than the knit stitch, to make garter stitch it is quicker to knit every row. Working this stitch produces a much denser fabric than stocking stitch.

BOTTOM LEFT **SINGLE RIB STITCH** - single rib is formed by knitting one stitch, purling the next stitch and repeating this sequence to the end of the row. The columns of knit and purl stitches are maintained in all the subsequent rows. Rib can be worked in varying combinations of knit and purl stitches, including k2, p2 and k2, p1.

BOTTOM RIGHT **MOSS STITCH** – this is worked in the same way as single rib in that you knit one stitch and then purl the next stitch and continue throughout the row. The difference is if you end a row with a purl stitch when knitting in single rib you start the next row with a knit stitch. When knitting moss stitch, if you finish a row with a purl stitch, you start the next row with a purl stitch, then continue in the P1, K1 pattern to the end of the row.

COMBINATION STITCHES

STOCKING STITCH

GARTER STITCH

MOSS STITCH

SINGLE RIB STITCH

CASTING OFF

"Casting off is the term used for finishing a piece of knitting by taking it off the needles. In order that the work does not unravel, the stitches must be securely cast off. Whether you knit with a 'tight' or 'loose' tension, keep your stitches looser than you usually would when casting off. This will stop the work from puckering at the cast-off edge. A tight cast-off can look ugly and will spoil your knitting. If you find it hard to keep your cast off loose, try using a knitting needle slightly bigger than you used in the rest of your knitting (in your right hand) to cast off with."

STEP 1 When casting off knitwise, knit two stitches in the usual way.

STEP 2 Insert the tip of the left-hand needle into the front of the first of these two knitted stitches.

STEP 6 Loosen the final stitch to make a bigger loop and remove the knitting needle.

STEP 7 Pass the cut end of the working yarn through this last loop.

STEP 8 Pull the yarn end to tighten the final loop and secure the last row of your knitted piece.

STEP 3 Carefully lift the first knitted stitch over the second and over the tip of the right-hand needle. Release the stitch you have just lifted over the right-hand needle from the tip of the left-hand needle.

STEP 4 You now have one stitch on the right-hand needle. Knit one more stitch so that you have two stitches on your right-hand needle again, then repeat the move of using the left-hand needle to lift the first stitch on the right-hand needle over the second stitch and off the needle. There should only be either one or two stitches on the right-hand needle at any point while casting off.

STEP 5 When you have been casting off for a full row and have one stitch left on the right-hand needle, cut the working yarn, leaving a fair length so your knitting doesn't unravel.

SHAPING WITH DECREASES

KNIT TWO STITCHES TOGETHER (K2TOG)

When shaping a garment you have to decrease and increase stitches the amount of stitches on your needles at different points so that you get a shape that fits nicely to the body. Often in knitting patterns you will find decreases three stitches in from the outside edge. This is called "fully fashioned shaping" and gives a neater result. This technique is very useful if you are working in one colour in a simple stitch such as stocking stitch. However, when working in a stitch pattern, such as a Fair Isle or a lace stitch, it can confuse the pattern repeat if you fully fashion, so you will just as often come across patterns that decrease right at the edge of the row.

"The easiest way to decrease the number of stitches in a row, is to knit two stitches together in one new stitch. This is as simple as it sounds. The abbreviation for this is k2tog which just means 'knit 2 together'. As with most things in knitting there are several ways to decrease stitches; this is the most straightforward – and most common – method."

STEP 1 When you are placing the tip of the right-hand needle into the stitches on the left-hand needle, instead of picking up just one stitch pick up the first two stitches at the same time.

STEP 2 Wind the yarn round the needle as you would with a normal knit stitch from back to front.

STEP 3 Catching the yarn that you've just wound round, bring the tip of the right-hand needle through the loops on the left-hand needle.

STEP 4 Then slide the two stitches off the left-hand needle to make one new stitch on the right-hand needle.

KNIT TWO STITCHES TOGETHER THROUGH BACK LOOPS (K2TOGTBL)

"This is another really simple way to decrease. It's very similar to k2tog, however you knit down into the back of the stitches instead. The abbreviation 'k2tog tbl' just means "knit 2 together through back loops"."

STEP 1 Instead of knitting up into the two stitches as you would do with a k2tog, place the tip of the right-hand needle down through the two stitches at the back of the work. Push the needle up further through the two stitches.

STEP 2 Wrap the yarn round the needle as you would with a normal knit stitch, from the back of the work to the front.

STEP 3 Catching the yarn that you've just looped round, pull the tip of the needle through both of the stitches being knitted together.

STEP 4 Slide both stitches off the left-hand needle leaving just one new stitch on the right-hand needle.

SHAPING WITH INCREASES

KNITTING INTO FRONT AND BACK OF ONE STITCH (KFB)

"When you increase within a row of knitting you can just cast on one stitch at the appropriate point, however this way of increasing gives a far neater finish and is often used in patterns for garments. With this increase method you knit into the front and back of a stitch, making two stitches from one stitch."

STEP 1 Insert the needle into the stitch as usual, wrap the yarn round and pull it through, but do not slip the loop off the needle. Keeping the new stitch on the right-hand needle, knit into the same stitch on the left-hand needle but into the back of the stitch.

STEP 2 Wrap the yarn round the right-hand needle as with any knit stitch, from back to front in an anti-clockwise motion.

STEP 3 Catch the yarn that has been wrapped round and bring the tip of the right-hand needle through the stitch.

STEP 4 Slide the new stitch off the left-hand needle. You now have two new stitches on the right-hand needle.

MAKE ONE (MI)

"If, within a knitting pattern, you are asked to increase with the instruction 'm1' this abbreviation means 'make one stitch'. The method for making the new stitch is the same whatever point within the row you are at."

STEP 1 With the tip of the left-hand needle, lift the horizontal bar between the unworked and worked stitches. If the picked-up loop is too tight to knit easily, loosen it with your fingers.

STEP 2 Knit this new loop from the left-hand needle as if it was a regular knit stitch.

STEP 3 When you count up the stitches at the end of this increase row, you will have one extra stitch.

JOINING IN A NEW BALL OF YARN

"When you come to the end of a ball of yarn, you will have to add a new ball in order to carry on knitting. It is exactly the same procedure as for adding a new colour to include a stripe in your knitting. It is best to make a colour change at the end of a row, so make sure you leave enough of a tail of the old yarn – at least 10cm – to fasten in the new yarn easily."

STEP 1 Make a cross shape with the new yarn under the old working yarn. Tie the new yarn into a loose knot, with the old yarn lying inside. Slide the new knot up until it touches the knitting needle. Pull both ends of the new yarn to tighten the knot.

STEP 2 Then simply start knitting with the new yarn as usual.

"Knitting a tension swatch before you start to knit a pattern is very important, especially if you are a beginner. The point of it is just to ensure that you are knitting in the same tension that the pattern is written in so you know that your garment will come out the right size and as the designer intended it."

If your tension matches that given at the beginning of the pattern, then your garment will knit up to the exact size required. Achieving an exact tension is really important when knitting garments, however is less vital for some projects in this book, such at the Striped Scarf on page 32 or the Hand Puff on page 48, because they do not need to fit the body closely.

The tension given at the beginning of a knitting pattern is almost always written giving the number of stitches in a 10 x 10cm square. It's best if you knit a few centimetres extra so that you can take a measurement from the middle of the swatch.

When you have a good sized swatch knitted up and laid out on a flat surface, take a tape measure and with some pins mark out a 10 x 10cm square and count the stitches within the pins. Each stitch looks like a 'V' and you will find generally that you will count more rows (vertically) than stitches (horizontally). This is because knit stitches are usually wider than they are tall. Once you have counted the stitches and the rows within this 10 x 10cm square you can compare your tension to that on the pattern. If it matches, that's great, you can begin to knit the pattern. If it doesn't match, don't worry. If you find that you have more stitches within the 10cm than the pattern states this means that you are knitting a little too tightly and so should try knitting another tension swatch using slightly thicker needles. If you find that you have fewer stitches within the 10cm then this means that you are knitting a little too loosely and so should try knitting another tension swatch using slightly thinner needles. It may seem a little painstaking to begin with, but it's definitely worth getting right.

SEWING AN INVISIBLE SEAM

MATTRESS STITCH

"Mattress stitch is a method of sewing up that gives an almost invisible finish when worked on stocking stitch, though it can be used on other knit stitches as well. I use it for virtually everything I knit now because I love the way that as you stitch you have the right sides of the knitting facing up, so as you work you are aware of how the knitting will look on the outside."

STEP 1 Lay out the pieces to be joined with right sides face up. Thread a darning needle or bodkin with the sewing up yarn. Anchor the sewing yarn to both pieces by passing the needle up through the right side piece and down through the left side piece.

STEP 2 In between each stitch, there is a horizontal 'bar' that links the two stitches. Insert your darning needle upwards underneath the first two bars in between the columns of stitches at the right side edge.

STEP 3 Insert the needle upwards underneath the corresponding two bars on the left side edge. Keep working in this way, alternating between right and left sides, hooking the needle under two bars at a time until all have been stitched.

STEP 4 After you've sewn up a few bars on each side, pull tightly on both ends of the sewing yarn to bring the two sides being sewn together. By tightening the seam, the very edge stitches are turned to the back of the work, leaving a slight ridge.

STEP 5 Once pulled tight, the yarn will effectively disappear as the pieces of knitting are brought together to create a very neat and virtually invisible seam from the outside. Weave in any yarn ends into the ridge on the reverse side of the work.

FIXING DROPPED STITCHES

"If you've dropped a stitch and it has started to 'ladder' the most important thing to do is not to panic. It is important to try and fix the dropped stitch as soon as you notice it."

STEP 1 Lay the work flat so you can see the dropped stitch clearly as well as all the strands of the rows above the dropped stitch. If the dropped stitch is within stocking stitch, it is easier to fix this with the knit side of the work facing.

STEP 2 Insert the crochet hook into the dropped stitch from the front to the back, keeping the ladder behind the dropped stitch. Hook the crochet hook onto the ladder behind the dropped stitch and pull it through to the front of the dropped stitch.

STEP 3 Keep climbing the ladder through each dropped stitch until you get back to the current row of knitting.

STEP 4 When there are no more ladders, put the final dropped stitch onto the left-hand needle and continue to work the row.

UNDOING STITCHES

"If you've just noticed that you've gone wrong only a few stitches back, then you can easily unravel a few stitches and move them back onto your left-hand needle from your right-hand needle. You can use this method to undo many rows of knitting – it is slow but methodical."

STEP 1 When undoing a stitch with a knit row facing, hold the working yarn to the back. Insert the right-hand needle from the back to the front into the stitch one row below the last stitch on the left-hand needle.

STEP 2 Slide the stitch off the tip of the left-hand needle, keeping the stich below on the right-hand needle.

STEP 3 Gently pull the working yarn to free the loop of the below stitch on the right-hand needle. Continue in this way until you have reached your mistake. When undoing a stitch with a purl row facing, hold the working yarn to the front of the work.

UNRAVELLING ROWS

"Every knitter makes a mistake from time to time, and sometimes mistakes go unnoticed even after a few more rows have been worked. This method is the quickest way to unravel – or 'rip out' – the rows to take you back to the good row preceding the mistake."

STEP 1 Thread a needle with coloured yarn. Identify the preceding good row of knitting and, with the right side up and working from right to left, pass the needle down through the centre 'V' of one stitch and then up through the centre 'V' of the next.

STEP 2 Continue in this way across the row of knitting until all the stitches are caught by the coloured yarn. Slide the knitting needle out of all the stitches at the top of the work so that the loops are free and the rows are ready to be unravelled.

STEP 3 Steadily unravel the knitting one row at a time by gently pulling the working yarn until each of the stitches disappear.

STEP 4 Unravel the knitting until you reach the row threaded with coloured yarn. This yarn holds all the stitches in the row and stops them from further unravelling. To stop the working yarn becoming tangled, wind all the unravelled yarn back onto the ball.

STEP 5 Thread the stitches back onto the needle from the opposite side to where the working yarn is sitting, so the tip of the needle ends up next to the working yarn. Count the stitches on the needle before removing the safety line of coloured yarn.

WORKING A
CABLE BACKWARD

"A cable is a twisted column of stitches, whereby the order in which the stitches are knitted is altered by using a short cable needle. Working a backwards cable creates and right slanting twist, while working a forwards cable creates a left slanting twist. Once you learn how to create a basic twist, you can experiment and knit all sorts of cable patterns."

The following instructions are for 'C4B' or 'cable four stitches backwards'. This instruction indicates that the width of the whole cable is four stitches wide and that the cable will be twisting over from left to right.

STEP 1 When you reach the row in which the cable twist is worked, work to the column of stitches that is to form the cable.

STEP 2 Slide the correct number of knit stitches (in this case, two stitches) onto the cable needle. The knitting pattern will include instructions on how many stitches are worked within the cable.

STEP 3 Place the cable needle and these two stitches at the back of the work. Knit the next two stitches directly from the left-hand needle.

STEP 4 Slip the first two stitches from the cable needle back on to the left-hand needle.

STEP 5 Knit these two stitches as usual now they are back on the left-hand needle. Continue as the pattern instructs. You will see how the cable twists over from left to right.

WORKING A CABLE FORWARD

"This cable forward is similar to knitting a cable backward, however instead of holding the cable needle at the back of the work, in this case you will be holding it at the front of the work. The following instructions are for 'C4F' or cable four stitches forward. This instruction indicates that the width of the whole cable is four stitches wide and the cable will be twisting over from right to left."

STEP 1 When you reach the row in which the cable twist is worked, work to the column of stitches that is to form the cable.

STEP 2 Slide the correct number of knit stitches (in this case, two stitches) onto the cable needle. Place the cable needle and these two stitches at the front of the work.

STEP 3 Knit the next two stitches directly from the left-hand needle.

STEP 4 Slip the first two stitches back on to the left-hand needle from the cable needle.

STEP 5 Knit these two stitches as usual now they are back on the left hand needle. Continue as the pattern instructs. You will see how the cable twists over from right to left.

learn TO KNIT

STRIPED SCARF AND MITTENS
WITH GIANT POMPOMS

 *learn*

SIZE
SCARF: One size, 200cm long by 15cm wide
MITTENS: One size, to fit average size woman's hands

YOU WILL NEED
A   2 x 100g hanks of superbulky weight wool yarn, such as Quince & Co Puffin, in orange (Apricot)
B   2 x 100g hanks of aran weight wool yarn, such as Malabrigo Merino Worsted, in mid pink (Dusty) – this yarn is used double throughout
Pair each of size 8mm and 10mm knitting needles
Two 8cm and two 6cm cardboard discs and pair of scissors
Tapestry needle

TENSION
12 stitches and 16 rows to 10cm square measured over stocking stitch using 10mm knitting needles and yarn A single and yarn B double throughout. However, as the scarf is a simple long knitted strip, it isn't strictly essential that your tension matches the recommended tension given here. Knitting any scarf is a really good way to practice your basic knit stitches as there is no shaping involved and it doesn't have to be an exact size. As you knit you will become comfortable with the stitch, and you will have a really lovely accessory once you are finished. If you decide to make the mittens to go with your scarf, it is more important to achieve a correct tension so that your mittens will fit well and won't either be too small or resemble an oven glove.

ABBREVIATIONS
See standard abbreviations on page 7.

" **WHILE KNITTING THE LONG SCARF,** I simply made up the stripe pattern as I worked. I varied the blocks of colour by making some stripes very wide and then interspersed a few narrower stripes made up of only one or two rows. You can do the same and just change colour whenever you feel like it. Bear in mind, however, that if you decide to follow your own stripe pattern then you may need more of one colour yarn."

TO MAKE THE SCARF

Using A and 10mm needles, cast on 18 sts.

ROW I (RS): K to end of row.

ROW 2: P to end of row.

These last two rows form the stocking stitch (st st) pattern, which is worked throughout.

Beg with a k row, cont to work in st st and stripes as folls:

A	34 rows	B	44 rows
B	22 rows	A	14 rows
A	8 rows	B	6 rows
B	4 rows	A	40 rows
A	6 rows	B	4 rows
B	18 rows	A	6 rows
A	12 rows	B	2 rows
B	2 rows	A	4 rows
A	4 rows	B	12 rows
B	2 rows	A	2 rows
A	26 rows	B	4 rows
B	22 rows	A	14 rows
A	6 rows	B	22 rows

Cast off loosely knitwise.

Make two pompoms (see opposite) using 8cm circles of cardboard, one in A to stitch to the pink end of the scarf and one in B to stitch to the orange end of the scarf.

TO MAKE THE LEFT MITTEN

Using A and 8mm needles, cast on 24 sts.

ROW I: * K1, p1; rep from * to end of row.

ROW 2: * K1, p1; rep from * to end of row.

These two rows form the single rib (k1, p1 rib) pattern.

Cont to work in single rib for a further 6 rows.

ROW I: K to end of row.

ROW 2: P to end of row.

These two rows form the stocking stitch (st st) pattern.

Beg with a k row, cont to work in st st and stripes as folls:

A	4 rows
B	4 rows

SHAPE THUMB

NEXT ROW (RS): K12, turn, cast on 6 sts, p12, turn.

Cont to work on these 12 sts only, leaving rem 6 sts on needle.

Cont to work in st st for a further 10 rows.

NEXT ROW: [K2tog] 6 times. *6 sts.*

Break yarn, leaving a long tail to stitch up thumb.

Thread yarn end through rem 6 sts, pull up tight and stitch thumb closed.

With RS facing, rejoin yarn at base of thumb and pick up 6 sts, k to end of row.

P 1 row.

Beg with a k row, cont to work in st st and stripes as folls:

B	10 rows
A	10 rows

NEXT ROW: [K2tog] 12 times.

NEXT ROW: [P2tog] 6 times.

Break yarn, leaving a long tail to stitch up side seam.

Thread yarn end through rem 6 sts, pull up tight and stitch side seam closed.

To make up, weave in any loose yarn ends.

TO MAKE THE RIGHT MITTEN

Using B and 8mm needles, cast on 24 sts.

Work 8 rows in single rib (k1, p1 rib) as given for Left Mitten.

Beg with a k row, cont in st st and stripes as folls:

B	4 rows
A	2 rows
B	4 rows

SHAPE THUMB

Change to A.

NEXT ROW: K18, turn, cast on 6 sts, p12, turn.

Cont working on these 12 sts only.

Work a further 10 rows in st st.

NEXT ROW: [K2tog] 6 times. *6 sts.*

Break yarn, leaving a long tail to stitch up thumb.

Thread yarn end through rem 6 sts, pull up tight and stitch thumb closed.

With RS facing, rejoin yarn at base of thumb and pick up 6 sts, knit to end of row.

P 1 row.

Beg with a k row, cont in st st and stripes as folls:

B	4 rows
A	2 rows
B	4 rows
A	2 rows
B	8 rows

NEXT ROW: [K2tog] 12 times. *12 sts.*

NEXT ROW: [P2tog] 6 times. *6 sts.*

Break yarn, leaving a long tail to stitch up side seam.

Thread yarn end through rem 6 sts, pull up tight and stitch side seam closed.

To make up, weave in any loose yarn ends.

Make two pompoms (see opposite) using 6cm circles of cardboard, one in A to stitch to right mitten and one in B to stitch to left mitten.

MAKING POMPOMS

"Quick and fun to make, a playful pompom can transform an otherwise plain scarf. The more wraps you make around the cardboard ring, the fuller the finished result will be, so it is worth taking a bit more time – and yarn – to create showstopping pompom."

STEP 1 Cut two circles of cardboard then cut a smaller concentric circle out of the centre of both card circles to make a ring.

STEP 2 Holding both cardboard circles together, start wrapping the yarn around the ring. You can thread the yarn onto a tapestry needle, which makes this process slightly quicker. As one length of yarn runs out, add in a new length.

STEP 3 Continue wrapping the yarn around the cardboard ring until it is completely covered. The more yarn you wrap around the ring, the fuller the resulting pompom will be.

STEP 4 Make a gap in the wrapped yarn and insert a blade of the scissors so it sits between the two cardboard rings. Keeping the scissors between the two cardboard rings, cut the wrapped yarn taking care not to lose any pieces of yarn from the ring.

STEP 5 Once the wrapped yarn has been cut, slide a length of yarn between the cardboard rings and wrap it tightly around the centre of the cut threads. Ease off the card. Pull the tie and make a tight knot, leaving a long tail. Trim any untidy threads.

SHOPPER
WITH DROPPED
STITCH DETAIL

 learn

SIZE
One size

YOU WILL NEED
1 x 500g cone of superbulky yarn, such as Hoopla Yarn
  Jersey, in red (Bright Red)
12mm circular needles, 80cm long
12mm crochet hook
60cm strong cotton tape (optional)

"**THIS SHOPPER IS
THE PERFECT PROJECT**
to practice working in the round as
it doesn't matter if your tension is a
little tight or a little loose because this
one-size bag fits all."

TENSION
Achieving an exact tension is not vital when knitting this
bag, as the finished size of the shopper can vary.

ABBREVIATIONS
See standard abbreviations on page 7.

CASTING ON WITH
CIRCULAR NEEDLES

"Always choose the correct
length of circular needle to
suit the number of stitches
being cast on. It is preferable
to have a lot of stitches on a
shorter wire as you can always
bunch the stitches together.
Too few stitches on a circular
needle and they will become
stretched. Before casting on, if
the nylon wire of your circular
needle appears twisted, dip it
in hot water and then pull the
wire to straighten."

STEP 1 Cast on the correct number
of stitches, make sure that all the
stitches are sitting straight on the
needles and wire and check that there
are no twists in the line of stitches.

STEP 2 Knit the first stitch on the
left hand point of the needle to join
the stitches into a round, make sure
that you pull the first stitch tight to
prevent a hole from forming.

TO MAKE THE BAG

Using size 12mm circular needles, cast on 56 sts (see instructions given on page 36 for casting on in the round). Working in the round, making sure you mark the beginning of each round so you know where the next round begins and ends, cont as folls:

ROUNDS 1, 2 AND 3: K to end of round. *

ROUND 4: Wrap yarn around needle four times when knitting each stitch to end of round.

NOTE: You will have lots and lots of loops on the wire of the circular needle as you have made four loops per knit stitch where ordinarily there would be only one.

ROUND 5: * Slide the first 8 sts off the LH needle and unravel all the loops so that you have eight long stitches, pass the first 4 sts through the loops of the next 4 sts and place them back onto the LH needle, knit these 8 sts as normal, rep from * to end of round.

(See instructions given opposite for working this dropped stitch pattern.)

ROUNDS 6, 7 AND 8: K to end of round.

Rep Rounds 4–8 one further time.

Rep Rounds 4–8 one further time but on Round 4 wrap the yarn around needle three times.

Rep Rounds 4–8 one further time but on Round 4 wrap the yarn around needle two times.

SHAPE BASE

ROUND 1: * K3, sl2, k1, p2sso, k2; rep from * to end of round. *42 sts.*

ROUND 2 AND ALL EVEN-NUMBERED ROUNDS: K to end of round.

ROUND 3: * K2, sl2, k1, p2sso, k1; rep from * to end of round. *28 sts.*

ROUND 5: * K1, sl2, k1, p2sso; rep from * to end of round. *14 sts.*

ROUND 7: * K2tog; rep to end of round. *7 sts.*

Break yarn, leaving a long tail. Thread yarn end through rem 7 sts, pull up tight and fasten off.

Weave in any loose yarn ends into the wrong side of the finished knitting.

TO MAKE THE BAG HANDLES

NOTE: A chain of crochet makes the strongest handles for this type of bag, as they can carry a lot of weight. However, if you prefer not to work the handles in crochet, then use lengths of strong cotton tape instead.

TO MAKE CROCHETED HANDLES

Using a 12mm crochet hook, pick up 13 sts at any point around open edge of shopper, make 18 chain, skip 15 sts along open edge of shopper, pick up another 13 sts and make 18 chain.

Work 1 round of double crochet on these 62 sts.

Break yarn. Weave in loose yarn ends.

TO MAKE SEWN HANDLES

Cut two 30cm lengths of strong cotton tape – one for each handle.

Pin the ends of each length of cotton tape to the inside rim of the open edge of the shopper.

Stitch in place with reinforced stitching, working a rectangle with a cross inside, at each end of the handle.

"This shopper is really quick to knit partly due to the chunky yarn it is worked in, which is available in a multitude of colours, but also because of the dropped stitch method used. After knitting so many projects where you must try to avoid dropping stitches, it's very refreshing and fun to work in this technique where holes in your work are a good thing."

WORKING THE DROPPED STITCH

STEP 1 When knitting the dropped stitch, insert the right-hand needle into the first stitch on the left-hand needle, wrap the yarn around the needle the number of times specified – either four, three or two – instead of the usual once.

STEP 2 Finish knitting the stitch in the usual way by bringing the needle through to the front and sliding the stitch off the left-hand needle.

STEP 3 On the next round, when you reach the dropped stitch, unravel the loops from the left-hand needle to give one long loop.

STEP 4 For this particular pattern, eight dropped stitches are worked in a group and you need to unravel all eight long loops at the same time. Once unraveled, divide the eight long loops into two groups of four.

STEP 5 Pass the first set of four long loops through the centre of the second four long loops to form a cross.

STEP 6 Keeping the stitches in this order, slide them back on to the left-hand needle and knit these eight loops in the usual way.

WRISTWARMERS
WITH CONTRAST RIB

learn

SIZE
One size, to fit average size woman's hand

YOU WILL NEED
Double-knitting weight wool yarn, such as Blue Sky
    Alpaca Melange or Blue Sky Alpaca Sport Weight, in the
    following colours (amounts given below will make one
    pair of wristwarmers):

FOR COLOURWAY ONE
A 1 x 50g hank in orange (Melange, Saffron)
B 1 x 50g hank in mustard (Melange, Dijon)

FOR COLOURWAY TWO
A 1 x 50g hank in mauve (Melange, Bubblegum)
B 1 x 50g hank in bright pink (Sport Weight, Hibiscus)

FOR COLOURWAY THREE
A 1 x 50g hank in pale blue (Sport Weight, Capri)
B 1 x 50g hank in pale grey (Sport Weight, Light Gray)

FOR COLOURWAY FOUR
A 1 x 50g hank in mustard (Melange, Dijon)
B 1 x 50g hank in mid blue (Sport Weight, Bluejay)

Pair each of size 3.25mm and 3.75mm knitting needles
Tapestry needle

TENSION
26 sts and 34 rows to 10cm square measured over
stocking stitch using 3.75mm knitting needles. Adjust
needle size as necessary to obtain tension.

ABBREVIATIONS
See standard abbreviations on page 7.

TO MAKE THE WRISTWARMERS (MAKE TWO)
Using 3.25mm needles and A, cast on 42 sts.
Change to B.
ROW 1 (RS): * K2, p2; rep from * to last 2 sts, k2.
ROW 2: * P2, k2; rep from * to last 2 sts, p2.
These two rows form the double rib (k2, p2 rib) pattern.
Cont to work in double rib for a further 12 rows, ending
with a WS row.
Change to 3.75mm needles.
NEXT ROW (RS): K to end of row.
NEXT ROW: P to end of row.
These two rows form the stocking stitch (st st) pattern.
Cont to work in st st until the Wristwarmer measures
20cm from cast-on edge, ending with a WS row.
Change to 3.25mm needles and yarn A.
NEXT ROW (RS): K to end of row.
NEXT ROW: * P2, k2; rep from * to last 2 sts, p2.
NEXT ROW: * K2, p2; rep from * to last 2 sts, k2.
Cont to work in double rib as set for a further 12 rows.
Cast off loosely in double rib.

TO MAKE UP
Fold the Wristwarmer in half widthways, with the wrong
sides facing, to form a tube.
Starting from the cast-on edge and working upwards, join
the first 18cm of the side edges using mattress stitch (see
instructions given on page 24) with B.
Leaving a gap of approximately 2cm for the thumbhole,
join the last 4cm of the side edges using mattress stitch
with A to match the contrast colour rib.

HIS OR HERS BOBBLE HATS

SIZE
One size, to fit average size man's or woman's head

YOU WILL NEED
Bulky weight wool yarn, such as Blue Sky Alpaca Bulky, in
the following colours:

FOR COLOURWAY ONE
A 1 x 100g hank of mustard (Bulky, Curry)
B 2 x 100g hanks of bright pink (Bulky, Azalea)

FOR COLOURWAY TWO
A 1 x 100g hank of cream (Bulky, Angora)
B 2 x 100g hanks of mid grey (Bulky, Gray Wolf)

10mm circular knitting needle (40cm long)
Two 8cm cardboard discs and pair of scissors
Tapestry needle

TENSION
10 stitches and 13 rows to 10cm square using 10mm
knitting needles over double rib (k2, p2 rib) when fabric
is slightly stretched. Adjust needle size as necessary to
obtain tension.

ABBREVIATIONS
S2TOGKPO slip 2 stitches together, knit 1, pass 2 slipped
stitches over
See also standard abbreviations on page 7.

> **" TIP**: weaving any loose yarn ends in
> vertically along the columns of stitches
> –rather than horizontally across a row
> of stitches – will help to keep the knitted
> rib elastic.**"**

TO MAKE THE HAT
Using 10mm circular needle and A, cast on 48 sts
(see instructions given on page 36).
Working in the round, marking the beg of each round
with a stitch marker or loop of contrast colour yarn,
cont as folls:
ROUND I: * K2, p2; rep from * to end of round.
The last round forms the double rib (k2, p2 rib) pattern.
Cont to work in double rib as set until Hat measures 10cm
from cast-on edge.
Change to B and cont to work in double rib as set until
Hat measures 25cm from cast-on edge.
Divide the stitches on the circular needle into six equal
groups, each containing 8 sts. Mark the beg and end of
each group with a stitch marker or loop of contrast
colour yarn.

SHAPE CROWN
ROUND I: * K2, p1, s2togkpo, p2; rep from * to end of
round. *36 sts.*
ROUND 2: * K2, p1, k1, p2; rep from * to end of round.
ROUND 3: * K2, s2togkpo, p1; rep from * to end of round.
24 sts.
ROUND 4: * K2, p2; rep from * to end of round.
ROUND 5: * K1, s2togkpo; rep from * to end of round.
12 sts.
ROUND 6: K to end of round.
ROUND 7: * K2tog; rep from * to end of round. *6 sts.*
Break yarn, leaving a long tail. Pass the yarn end through
the rem 6 sts and fasten off.

TO FINISH
Weave any loose yarn ends into the wrong side of the
finished knitting.
Make a pompom using 8cm circles of cardboard in A
(see instructions given on page 35).
Stitch securely to the top of the hat.

"THESE UNISEX
BOBBLE HATS are knitted
in double rib and simply shaped
by working decreases over the
last few rounds. The rib creates a
stretchy fabric, so this pattern fits
a variety of head sizes."

HAND PUFF
AND COLLAR
WITH EMBROIDERY

learn

SIZE
One size

YOU WILL NEED
MC 2 x 100g balls of superbulky weight bouclé wool yarn, such as Rowan Purelife British Sheeps Breed Bouclé, in mid grey-brown (Light Brown Masham)

FOR SURFACE EMBROIDERY
Oddments of double-knitting weight wool yarn, such as Jamieson's Double Knitting Shetland Wool, in the following colours:

A deep red (Cherry)
B turquoise (Splash)
C mid green (Verdigris)
D pale green (Apple)
E gold-green (Bracken)
F bright pink (Fuchsia)

Pair of size 8mm knitting needles, for collar
8mm circular knitting needle, 50cm long, for hand puff
Tapestry needle
55cm x 30cm piece of thick cotton wadding
55cm x 34cm piece of lining fabric in a complementary colour or print
Matching sewing thread
250cm length and 10cm length of striped narrow grosgrain ribbon, 6mm wide
One button, 2cm in diameter

TENSION
10 sts and 16 rows to 10cm square using 8mm knitting needles over moss stitch pattern. Adjust needle size as necessary to obtain tension.

ABBREVIATIONS
See also standard abbreviations on page 7.

"JUST THE THING TO BRIGHTEN UP A WINTER COAT, this Hand Puff and Collar duo can be made in as little as one evening. Worked in superbulky yarn, the moss stitch pattern is quick to work once you get into the rhythm of knit one stitch, purl one stitch. I have chosen a bouclé yarn for a very textured finish and – as this yarn softens the stitch definition – it is also quite forgiving if you happen to go wrong. Surface embroidery is a great way to introduce colour into your knitting, without having to use any special techniques."

TO MAKE THE HAND PUFF

Using 8mm circular needle and MC, cast on 50 sts (see instructions given on page 36).
Working in the round, marking the beg of each round with a stitch marker or loop of contrast colour yarn, cont as folls:
ROUND 1: * K1, p1; rep from * to end of round.
ROUND 2: * P1, k1; rep from * to end of round.
These two rounds form the moss stitch (moss st) pattern.
Cont to work in moss st as set until Hand Puff measures 28cm from cast-on edge.
Cast off loosely in moss st.

ADD SURFACE EMBROIDERY

Place the knitted tube in front of you with the open ends at the sides. Using backstitch and the oddments of contrast colour yarn, embroider additional criss-crossing diagonal lines over the surface of the Hand Puff, running from open edge to open edge, to form a 'tartan' pattern. You will need to rotate the Hand Puff as you embroider.

TO MAKE UP

Place the piece of cotton wadding inside the knitted tube and, if necessary, trim to fit.
Remove the wadding from inside the tube and use it to create a template for the lining fabric. Cut the lining fabric to the size of the wadding plus an extra 2cm to each side for the seam allowance.
With right sides together, sew the ends of the lining fabric together to make a tube.
With the wrong side out, place the wadding on top of the lining fabric tube, turn back the 2cm seam allowance of the lining fabric and tack the wadding and lining together.
Slide the wadding and lining inside the knitted tube, then neatly hand-sew the ends of the lining tube to the knitted tube with matching sewing thread.
Pass the 250cm length of narrow grosgrain ribbon through the Hand Puff and tie into a bow to create the neckstrap. Adjust the length of the ribbon until the Hand Puff is at the perfect height for you.

TO MAKE THE COLLAR

Using a pair of 8mm needles and MC, cast on 58 sts.
ROW 1: * K1, p1; rep from * to end of row.
ROW 2: * P1, k1; rep from * to end of row.
These two rows form the moss stitch (moss st) pattern.
Cont to work in moss st throughout, taking care to keep the stitch pattern correct when decreasing.
ROW 3: Patt 6, k2tog, patt 7, k2tog, patt 7, k2tog, patt 6, k2tog, patt 7, k2tog, patt 7, k2tog, patt 6. *52 sts.*
ROW 4: Work in moss st to end of row.
ROW 5: Patt 5, k2tog, patt 6, k2tog, patt 6, k2tog, patt 5, k2tog, patt 6, k2tog, patt 6, k2tog, patt 6. *46 sts.*
ROW 6: Work in moss st to end of row.
ROW 7: Patt 6, k2tog, patt 6, k2tog, patt 6, k2tog, patt 6, k2tog, patt 6, k2tog, patt 6. *41 sts.*
ROWS 8, 9 AND 10: Work in moss st to end of row.
Cast off loosely in moss st.

ADD SURFACE EMBROIDERY

Place the Collar flat in front of you. Using backstitch and the oddments of contrast colour yarn, embroider additional criss-crossing diagonal lines over the surface the Collar, as for the Hand Puff. However, as the Collar is smaller than the Hand Puff, you may prefer to add only one or two lines for a flash of colour.

TO MAKE UP

Fold the 10cm length of ribbon into a loop and pass the two ends through one top front edge of the Collar and knot at the back to secure.
Sew the button on to the opposite front edge to fasten.

SIMPLE ROUND NECK SWEATER
WITH RAGLAN SLEEVES

 *learn*

SIZE

UK	8	10	12	14	16
TO FIT BUST (CM)	81	86	91	97	102
TO FIT BUST (IN)	32	34	36	38	40
ACTUAL BUST (CM)	92	96	100	106	110
ACTUAL BUST (IN)	36¼	37¾	39½	41¾	43¼
LENGTH (CM)	59.5	60	62	63	63.5
LENGTH (IN)	23½	23¾	22½	23½	24
SLEEVE SEAM (CM)	43	43	43	44	44
SLEEVE SEAM (IN)	17	17	17	17½	17½

YOU WILL NEED

9 (10: 11: 12: 13) x 50g balls double-knitting weight
  wool yarn, such as Frog Tree Alpaca Sport Melange
  in coral (Coral)
Pair each of size 3mm and 3.75mm needles
Tapestry needle

TENSION

24 sts and 32 rows to 10cm square measured over
stocking stitch using 3.75mm needles. Adjust needle size
as necessary to obtain tension.

ABBREVIATIONS

SKPO slip 1 stitch, knit 1 stitch, pass slipped stitch over
SK2TOGPO slip 1 stitch, knit 2 stitches together, pass
slipped stitches over
See also standard abbreviations on page 7.

TO MAKE THE BACK

Using 3mm needles, cast on 111 (115: 121: 127: 133) sts.
ROW 1 (RS): * K1, p1; rep from * to last st, k1.
ROW 2 (WS): * P1, k1; rep from * to last st, p1.
The last two rows form the single rib (k1, p1 rib) pattern.
Cont to work in single rib as set until Back measures 4cm
from cast-on edge, ending with a WS row.
Change to 3.75mm needles.
ROW 1 (RS): K to end of row.
ROW 2 (WS): P to end of row.
The last two rows form the stocking stitch (st st) pattern.
Cont to work in st st until Back measures 37.5 (37.5: 38.5:
38.5: 38.5)cm from cast-on edge, ending with a WS row.

SHAPE RAGLANS

Cast off 5 sts at beg of next 2 rows.
101 (105: 111: 117: 123) sts.
Cont to work in st st without shaping for a further 2 rows.
ROW 1: K3, skpo, k to last 5 sts, k2tog, k3.
ROW 2: P to end of row.
The last two rows set the position of decs for raglan
shaping.
Rep Rows 1 and 2 a further 3 times, working decs as set.
93 (97: 103: 109: 115) sts.
Cont to work in st st without shaping for a further 2 rows.
Rep Rows 1 and 2 a further 4 times, working decs as set.
85 (89: 95: 101: 107) sts.
Cont to work in st st without shaping for a further 2 rows.
Rep Rows 1 and 2 a further 3 times, working decs as set.
79 (83: 89: 95: 101) sts.
Cont to work in st st without shaping for a further 2 rows.
Rep Rows 1 and 2 a further 5 times, working decs as set.
69 (73: 79: 85: 91) sts.

> **"TIP:** for a neat even neckband, it easier to pick up fewer stitches
> over a smaller area, so divide up the neck edge into sections. For
> example, rather than trying to pick up 16 sts evenly along the left
> front neck in one go, break it down into four sets of four stitches."

ROW 3: K3, sk2togpo, k to last 6 sts, k3tog, k3.
ROW 4: P to end of row.
65 (69: 75: 81: 87) sts.
**
Rep Rows 3 and 4 one further time.
Rep Rows 1 and 2 one further time.
Rep Rows 3 and 4 a further 3 (3: 3: 3: 4) times.
Rep Rows 1 and 2 a further 1 (1: 2: 3: 3) times.
Rep Rows 3 and 4 a further 2 (3: 3: 4: 4) times.
Rep Row 1 one further time.
NEXT ROW (WS): P3, p2tog, p to last 5 sts, p2tog tbl, p3.
Rep Row 1 one further time.
NEXT ROW (WS): P3, p2tog, p to last 5 sts, p2tog tbl, p3.
Cast off rem 29 (29: 33: 33: 35) sts.

TO MAKE THE FRONT
Work as given for Back to **.
65 (69: 75: 81: 87) sts.

SHAPE NECK
NEXT ROW (RS): K3, sk2togpo, k until there are
23 (25: 28: 31: 34) sts on RH needle, turn, leave rem
unworked sts on a stitch holder.
Work each side of next separately.
Work left side of neck on these 23 (25: 28: 31: 34) sts
only as folls:
NEXT ROW (WS): Cast off 2 sts at neck edge, p to end
of row. *21 (23: 26: 29: 32) sts.*
ROW 1: K3, skpo, k to end of row.
ROW 2: P2tog, p to end of row. *19 (21: 24: 27: 30) sts.*
ROW 3: K3, sk2togpo, knit to end.
ROW 4: P2tog, p to end of row.
Rep Rows 3 and 4 one further time.
13 (15: 18: 21: 24) sts.

FOR SIZE 16 ONLY
Rep Rows 3 and 4 one further time. *21 sts.*

FOR SIZES 8 AND 10 ONLY
ROW 1: K3, skpo, k to end of row.
ROW 2: P to end of row. *11 (13: –: –: –) sts.*

FOR SIZE 12 ONLY
ROW 1: K3, skpo, k to end of row.
ROW 2: P2tog, p to end of row.
ROW 3: K3, skpo, k to end of row.
ROW 4: P to end of row. *– (–: 13: –: –) sts.*

FOR SIZES 14 AND 16 ONLY
ROW 1: K3, skpo, k to end of row.

ROW 2: P to end of row.
ROW 3: K3, skpo, k to end of row.
ROW 4: P to end of row. *– (–: –: 17: 17) sts.*

FOR SIZES 8, 10, 14 AND 16 ONLY
ROW 1: K3, skpo, k to end of row.
ROW 2: P2tog, p to end. *9 (11: –: 15: 15) sts.*

FOR ALL SIZES
ROW 3: K3, sk2togpo, k to end of row.
ROW 4: P to end of row.
Rep the last two rows until 5 sts rem.
NEXT ROW (RS): K3, skpo.
NEXT ROW: P2tog, p2.
NEXT ROW: K1, skpo.
NEXT ROW: P2tog.
Fasten off.
With RS of work facing, rejoin yarn to sts from stitch
holder.
NEXT ROW: Cast off 15 sts, k to last 6 sts, k3tog, k3.
Work right side of neck to match left side of neck,
reversing all shaping.
NOTE: Remember to work k2tog instead of skpo for
raglan decs worked on a RS row, work k3tog instead of
sk2togpo for raglan double decs worked on a RS row and
work p2togtbl instead of p2tog for raglan decs worked on
a WS row.

TO MAKE THE SLEEVE (MAKE TWO)
Using 3mm needles, cast on 51 (51: 53: 53: 55) sts.
ROW 1: * K1, p1; rep from * to last st, k1.
ROW 2: * P1, k1; rep from * to last st, p1.
The last two rows form the single rib (k1, p1 rib) pattern.
Cont to work in single rib until Sleeve measures 4cm from
the cast-on edge, ending with a WS row.
Change to 3.75mm needles.
ROW 1 (RS): K1, m1, k to last st, m1, k1.
ROWS 2, 4, 6 AND 8: P to end of row.
ROWS 3, 5, AND 7: K to end of row.
The last eight rows set the position of incs for sleeve shaping.
Rep the last eight rows until there are 81 (81: 83: 83: 85) sts.
Cont to work in st st without shaping until Sleeve
measures 43 (43: 43: 44: 44)cm from cast-on edge,
ending with a WS row.

SHAPE RAGLANS
Cast off 5 sts at beg of next 2 rows. *71 (71: 73: 73: 75) sts.*
ROWS 1 AND 3: K3, skpo, k to last 5 sts, k2tog, k3.
ROWS 2 AND 4: P to end of row.

ROW 5: K3, sk2togpo, k to last 6 sts, k3tog, k3.
ROW 6: P to end of row.
Rep Rows 1–6 a further four times.
Rep Rows 1 and 2 a further four times.
Rep Row 1 one further time.
Cont to work in st st without shaping for a further 3 rows.
21 (21: 23: 23: 25) sts.
Rep Rows 1 and 2 a further 1 (1: 1: 1: 2) times.

FOR SIZES 10, 14 AND 16 ONLY
Cont to work in st st without shaping for a further 2 rows.

FOR ALL SIZES
Rep Row 1.
Cont to work in st st without shaping for a further 3 rows.
Rep the last four rows a further 3 (3: 4: 4: 4) times.

FOR SIZES 14 AND 16 ONLY
Cont to work in st st without shaping for a further 2 rows.

FOR ALL SIZES
NEXT ROW (RS): K3, skpo, k1, k2tog, k3.
NEXT ROW: P to end of row.
Cast off rem 9 sts.

TO MAKE UP
Weave in any loose yarn ends.
Join each Front shaped raglan edge to a shaped raglan edge of a Sleeve.
Join the Back right shaped raglan edge to the left shaped raglan edge of a Sleeve.
Leave the Back left raglan edge open.

WORK NECKBAND
With RS facing and using 3mm needles, pick up and knit 9 sts from top of left sleeve, 16 sts down left side of front neck, 15 sts from front neck, 16 sts up right side of front neck, 9 sts from top of right sleeve and 29 (29: 33: 33: 35) sts along back neck. *94 (94: 98: 98: 100) sts.*
Work 6 rows in single rib.
Cast off loosely in rib.

TO FINISH
Join Back left shaped raglan edge to right shaped raglan edge of a Sleeve.
Join ends of the neckband.
Join side and sleeve seams using mattress stitch.

PICKING UP STITCHES FOR A NECKBAND

"It is possible to knit a neckband separately and then sew it in place, but I prefer to pick up stitches around the neck edge and knit on the neckband. This can be done using either straight needles or a circular needle."

STEP I Hold the working yarn at the back of the knitting. From the front of the work, insert the tip of the needle into the space between the edge stitch and next stitch. Wrap the working yarn around the needle, then bring the needle and yarn through to the right side of the work. Continue in this way until the required number of stitches have been picked up.

CROPPED CARDIGAN
WITH CABLED SLEEVES

SIZE

UK	8	10	12	14
TO FIT BUST (CM)	81	86	91	97
TO FIT BUST (IN)	32	34	36	38
ACTUAL BUST (CM)	87	92.5	98	103.5
ACTUAL BUST (IN)	34¼	36½	38½	40¾
SHORT VERSION (CM)	42.5	42.5	44.5	45.5
SHORT VERSION (IN)	16¾	16¾	17½	18
LONG VERSION (CM)	49.5	49.5	51.5	52.5
LONG VERSION (IN)	19½	19½	20¼	20¾
SLEEVE SEAM (CM)	37	37	38	38
SLEEVE SEAM (IN)	15	15	15½	15½

YOU WILL NEED

Double-knitting weight wool yarn, such as Juno Pearl DK
in the following colours:

FOR THE SHORT VERSION
4 (5: 6: 7) x 100g hanks in gold (Goldmine)

FOR THE LONG VERSION
4 (5: 6: 7) x 100g hanks in pale green (Fresh Greens)

Pair each of size 3.25mm and 4mm knitting needles
Cable needle
Stitch holder
Tapestry needle
6 or 8 buttons

TENSION

22 sts and 30 rows to 10cm square measured over stocking stitch using 4mm needles. Adjust needle size as necessary to obtain tension.

ABBREVIATIONS

BC back cross – slip one stitch onto cable needle, hold at back of work, knit two stitches, purl one stitch from cable needle

FC front cross – slip two stitches onto cable needle, hold at front of work, pur one stitch, knit two stitches from cable needle

LT left twist – with RH needle behind LH needle, skip first stitch and knit into back loop of second stitch, insert RH needle into backs of both stitches, knit two together through back loops

MK make knot – (k1, p1, k1, p1, k1, p1, k1) into next stitch, pass 2nd, 3rd, 4th, 5th, 6th and 7th sts on RH needle separately over last stitch made

RT right twist – knit two together leaving stitches on LH needle, insert RH needle from front between 2 stitches of k2tog, knit first stitch again, slip both stitches together from needle

See also standard abbreviations on page 7.

BRIAR ROSE PATTERN USED ON BACK AND FRONT (A 12-ROW REPEAT WORKED OVER 13 STS)

ROW I (WS): K3, p1, k1, p2, k2, p1, k3.
ROW 2: P3, LT, p1, LT, RT, p3.
ROW 3: K4, p2, k2, p1, k4.
ROW 4: P2, (k1, yo, k1) into next st, turn, p3, turn, k3 wrapping yarn twice round needle for each st, p1, LT, p1, RT, p4.
ROW 5: K4, p2, k1, p1, k2, sl next 3 sts dropping extra wraps, sl same 3 sts back onto LH needle, p3togtbl, k2.
ROW 6: P2, LT, p1, k1-b, RT, LT, p3.
ROW 7: K3, p1, k2, p2, k1, p1, k3.
ROW 8: P3, LT, RT, p1, RT, p3.
ROW 9: K4, p1, k2, p2, k4.
ROW I0: P4, LT, p1, RT, p1, (k1, yo, k1) into next st, turn, p3, turn, k3 wrapping yarn twice round needle for each st, p2.
ROW II: K2, sl next 3 sts dropping extra wraps, sl same 3 sts back onto LH needle, p3tog, k2, p1, k1, p2, k4.
ROW I2: P3, RT, LT, k1-b, p1, RT, p2.
Repeat Rows 1–12.

TO KNIT THE BACK
Using 3.25mm needles, cast on 96 (102: 108: 114) sts.

FOR 1ST AND 3RD SIZES ONLY
ROW I (RS): * K2, p2; rep from * to end of row.
ROW 2: * K2, p2; rep from * to end of row.

FOR 2ND AND 4TH SIZES ONLY
ROW I (RS): * K2, p2; rep from * to last 2 sts, k2.
ROW 2: *P2, k2; rep from * to last 2 sts, p2.

ALL SIZES
The last two rows form the double rib (k2, p2 rib) pattern. Cont to work in double rib as set for a further 20 rows. Change to 4mm needles.
ROW I (RS): K to end of row.
ROW 2 (WS): P to end of row.
The last two rows form the stocking stitch (st st) pattern. Cont to work in st st until Back measures 15 (15: 16: 17) cm for the short version or 22 (22: 23: 24)cm for the long version from cast-on edge, ending with a WS row.

SHAPE RAGLAN AND PLACE BRIAR ROSE PATTERN
NEXT ROW (RS): Cast off 4 sts knitwise, k to end of row.
NEXT ROW (WS): Cast off 4 sts purlwise (st on RH needle after cast off becomes selvedge st), work Row 1 of Briar Rose patt over 13 sts, p to last 14 sts, work Row 1 of Briar Rose patt, p1.

NOTE: The selvedge stitch is always a knit stitch on RS rows and a purl stitch on WS rows.
Cont to work Briar Rose patt on first and last 14 sts of each row but AT THE SAME TIME work raglan shaping by dec on 15th and 16th sts from beg and end of each row on next and every foll 4th row until 58 (70: 76: 88)sts rem. Work dec row as folls:
NEXT ROW (RS): K1, work Briar Rose patt over next 13 sts, skpo, k to 16th st from end of row, k2tog, work Briar Rose patt over next 13 sts, k1.
NOTE: The dec row is always a RS row and the decs are made just inside the Briar Rose patt.
NEXT ROW (WS): P1, work Briar Rose patt over next 13 sts, p to last 14 sts, work Briar Rose patt over next 13 sts, p1. Keeping Briar Rose patt correct, work decs as set on next and every foll alt row until 36 (36: 38: 38) sts rem.
NEXT ROW (WS): P1, work Briar Rose patt over next 13 sts, p to last 14 sts, work Briar Rose patt over next 13 sts, p1. Place rem sts on a stitch holder.

TO KNIT THE LEFT FRONT
With 3.25mm needles, cast on 47 (50: 53: 56) sts.

FOR 1ST SIZE ONLY
ROW I: P1, * k2, p2; rep from * to last 2 sts, k2.
ROW 2: * P2, k2; rep from * to last 3 sts, p2, k1.

FOR 2ND SIZE ONLY
ROW I: * K2, p2; rep from * to last 2 sts, k2.
ROW 2: * P2, k2; rep from * to last 2 sts, p2.

FOR 3RD SIZE ONLY
ROW I: K1, * p2, k2; rep from * to end of row.
ROW 2: * P2, k2; rep from * to last st, p1.

FOR 4TH SIZE ONLY
ROW I: * P2, k2; rep from * to end of row.
ROW 2: * P2, k2; rep from * to end of row.

ALL SIZES
The last two rows form the double rib (k2, p2 rib) pattern. Cont to work in double rib as set for a further 20 rows. Change to 4mm needles.
ROW I (RS): K to end of row.
ROW 2 (WS): P to end of row.
The last two rows form the stocking stitch (st st) pattern. Cont to work in st st until Left Front measures 15 (15: 16: 17)cm for the short version or 22 (22: 23: 24)cm for the long version from cast-on edge and matches Back to raglan, ending with a WS row.

SHAPE RAGLAN AND PLACE BRIAR ROSE PATTERN

NEXT ROW (RS): Cast off 4 sts knitwise, k to end of row.

NEXT ROW (WS): P to last 14 sts, work Row 1 of Briar Rose patt over next 13 sts, p1.

NOTE: The selvedge stitch is always a knit stitch on RS rows and a purl stitch on WS rows.

Cont to work the Briar Rose patt as set but AT THE SAME TIME work raglan shaping by dec on 15th and 16th sts on next and every foll 4th row until 28 (34: 37: 43) sts rem. Work dec row as folls:

NEXT ROW (RS): K1, work Briar Rose patt over next 13 sts, skpo, k to end of row.

NOTE: The dec row is always a RS row and the decs are made just inside the Briar Rose patt.

NEXT ROW (WS): P1, work Briar Rose patt over next 13 sts, p to end of row.

Keeping Briar Rose patt correct, work decs as set on next and every foll alt row until 25 (25: 28: 28) sts rem.

SHAPE NECK

NEXT ROW (WS): Cast off 7 (7: 8: 8) sts purlwise, p to end last 14 sts, work Briar Rose patt over next 13 sts, p1.

Keeping Briar Rose patt correct, dec 1 st at neck edge as set on next 8 rows but AT THE SAME TIME dec 1 st at raglan edge on next and every alt row until 6 (6: 8: 8) sts rem.

Keeping Briar Rose patt correct, dec 1 st at raglan edge on next and 2 (2: 4: 4) foll alt RS rows until 3 sts rem.

NEXT ROW (WS): Work 1 row.

NEXT ROW (RS): K1, skpo.

NEXT ROW (WS): P to end of row.

NEXT ROW (RS): Skpo.

Fasten off.

TO KNIT RIGHT FRONT

Work as given for Left Front, reversing all shaping and working k2tog instead of skpo for decs at raglan shaping.

HOLLOW OAK PATTERN USED ON SLEEVES (A 20-ROW REPEAT WORKED OVER 15 STS)

ROWS 1, 3, 5 AND 7 (WS): K5, p5, k5.
ROW 2: P5, k2, MK, k2, p5.
ROW 4: P5, MK, k3, MK, p5.
ROW 6: As Row 2.
ROW 8: P4, BC, p1, FC, p4.
ROW 9: K4, p2, k1, p1, k1, p2, k4.
ROW 10: P3, BC, k1, p1, k1, FC, p3.
ROW 11: K3, p3, k1, p1, k1, p3, k3.

ROW 12: P2, BC, (p1, k1) twice, p1, FC, p2.
ROW 13: K2, p2, [k1, p1] 3 times, k1, p2, k2.
ROW 14: P2, k3, (p1, k1) twice, p1, k3, p2.
ROWS 15: As Row 13.
ROW 16: P2, FC, (p1, k1) twice, p1, BC, p2.
ROW 17: As Row 11.
ROW 18: P3, FC, k1, p1, k1, BC, p3.
ROW 19: As Row 9.
ROW 20: P4, FC, p1, BC, p4.
Repeat Rows 1–20.

TO KNIT SLEEVES (MAKE TWO)

With 3.25mm needles, cast on 43 (43: 45: 45) sts.

ROW 1: K1, * p2, k2; rep from * to end of row.

ROW 2: * P2, k2; rep from * to last st, p1.

The last two rows for the double rib (k2, p2 rib) pattern.

Cont to work in double rib as set for a further 12 rows.

Change to 4mm needles.

Beg with a p row, work in st st with Hollow Oak patt over centre 15 sts but AT THE SAME TIME inc 1 st at both ends of first and every foll 4th row until 91 (91: 95: 95) sts.

Keeping st st and Hollow Oak patt correct, cont without shaping for a further 6 rows, ending with a p row.

SHAPE RAGLANS

Keeping st st and Hollow Oak patt correct, cast off 4 sts at beg of next 2 rows.

NEXT ROW (RS): K3, skpo, work to last 5 sts, k2tog, k3.

Keeping st st and Hollow Oak patt correct, dec at raglans as set on every foll 4th row until 71 (71: 75: 75) sts rem, ending with a WS row.

Keeping st st and Hollow Oak patt correct, cont to work decs at raglan edges as set on next and every foll alt row until 13 sts rem, ending with a WS row.

Place rem sts on a stitch holder.

NOTE: When Sleeve becomes narrow and there is no more st st, maintain raglan shaping by working decs in Hollow Oak patt. The first and last 5 sts of each row are worked in patt as set on RS rows and purled on WS rows.

YOU WILL HAVE COMPLETED:

1ST AND 2ND SIZES ONLY
9 complete Hollow Oak patt repeats + 1 extra row.

3RD AND 4TH SIZES ONLY
9 complete Hollow Oak patt repeats + 9 extra rows.

TO MAKE UP

Join the raglan edges of the Left and Right Fronts and Back to the raglan edges of the Sleeves.

WORK NECKBAND

With RS facing and 3.25mm needles, begin at Right Front pick up 20 (20: 23: 23) sts along right side of neck, 13 sts from top of right sleeve, 36 (36: 38: 38) sts from Back, 13 sts from top of left sleeve, then 20 (20: 23: 23) sts down left side of neck. *102 (102: 110: 110) sts.*

ROW I (RS): * K2, p2; rep from * to last 2 sts, k2.

ROW 2: *P2, k2; rep from * to last 2 sts, p2.

The last two rows form the double rib (k2, p2 rib) patt.

Cont to work in double rib until Neckband measures 3cm.

Cast off evenly in rib.

Join side and sleeve seams using mattress stitch.

WORK BUTTONBAND

With 3.25mm needles, cast on 10 sts.

Work in double rib as given for Neckband until buttonband streches up Left Front to top of Neckband. Cast off evenly in rib.

Slip stitch buttonband in place.

Mark position of 6 buttons for short version and 8 buttons for long version on Left Front buttonband. The lowest button must sit 1cm above bottom edge and the highest buttonhole must sit in the centre of the Neckband. Evenly space remaining buttons between these two.

BUTTONHOLE BAND

Work as given for buttonband but AT THE SAME TIME work buttonholes to correspond with marked positions on the buttonband (see instructions below).

Sew buttons securely onto buttonband to correspond with buttonholes.

"This versatile method of making buttonholes can be adapted according to the size of buttons you are using. Simply cast off more or fewer stitches to adjust the size of the buttonhole."

MAKING A BUTTONHOLE

STEP I On the first buttonhole row, work as usual to the buttonhole position. Work two stitches, then lift the first stitch over the second stitch to cast off one stitch. Repeat this until 4 stitches have been cast off.

STEP 2 Work to the end of the first buttonhole row as usual. On the next row, work to the position of the cast-off stitches on the previous row and then turn the work.

STEP 3 Using the cable cast on method (see page 11), cast on 4 stitches. Before placing the last cast-on stitch onto the left-hand needle, bring the yarn forward to the front. Turn and complete the row as usual.

LACE COLLAR
WITH TIE FASTENING

 *learn*

SIZE
One size (adjustable)

YOU WILL NEED
MC 2-ply laceweight wool yarn, such as Buffalo Gold Lux Lace or Natural Dye Studio Angel 2-ply Lace

A 2-ply laceweight cotton yarn, such as Fyberspates Scrumptious Lace or Habu Non-Twist Cotton Bouclé Lace

FOR COLOURWAY ONE:
MC 1 x 40g skein in dark green (Lux Lace, Pine)

A small amount in gold (Scrumptious Lace, Gold)

FOR COLOURWAY TWO:
MC 1 x 100g skein in pink (Angel 2-ply Lace, Bobby's Girl)

A small amount in pale green (Non-Twist Cotton Bouclé Lace, Aqua)

Pair each of 3mm and 3.5mm knitting needles
One self-cover button, 2.5cm diameter (optional)

TENSION
The 12-stitch lace pattern repeat measures approximately 6cm worked on 3mm needles. However, do not worry too much if your tension is not completely accurate as the collar is adjustable.

ABBREVIATIONS
See standard abbreviations on page 7.

TO MAKE LEFT SIDE OF COLLAR
Wind a length of yarn A into a small bobbin (see instructions given on page 90).

Using 3mm needles and A, cast on 61 sts using the lace cast-on method.

NOTE: For the lace cast-on method, pass the RH needle through the loop on the LH needle to form the new stitch, rather than between the loops.

K 3 rows.

Keeping 3 knit sts in A at each edge, twisting strands of A and MC together to avoid a hole, cont to work 12-row repeat lace patt as folls:

ROW 1: K3 in A, change to MC, k1, [k2tog, yf, k1, yf, k2tog tbl, k7] x 4 times, k2tog, yf, k1, yf, k2tog tbl, k1, join in bobbin of A, k3 in A.

ROW 2 AND ALL EVEN-NUMBERED ROWS: K3 in A, change to MC, p to last 3 sts, k3 in A.

ROW 3: K3 in A, change to MC, k2tog, [yf, k3, yf, k2tog tbl, k5, k2tog] x 4 times, yf, k3, yf, k2tog tbl, k3 in A.

ROW 5: As Row 1.

ROW 7: K3 in A, change to MC, k1, [k6, k2tog, yf, k1, yf, k2tog tbl, k1] x 4 times, k6, k3 in A.

ROW 9: K3 in A, change to MC, k1, [k5, k2tog, yf, k3, yf, k2tog tbl] x 4 times, k6, k3 in A.

ROW 11: As Row 11.

Change to 3.5mm needles and work 12-row repeat lace patt but AT THE SAME TIME working decs on front and back centre edges as folls:

ROW 1: K3 in A, change to MC, k1, [k2tog, yf, k1, yf, k2tog tbl, k7] x 4 times, k2tog, yf, k1, yf, k2tog tbl, k1, k3 in A.

ROW 2 AND ALL EVEN-NUMBERED ROWS: K3 in A, change to MC, p to last 3 sts, k3 in A.

ROW 3: K3 in A, change to MC, k2tog, k3, yf, k2tog tbl, k5, k2tog, [yf, k3, yf, k2tog tbl, k5, k2tog] x 3 times, yf, k3, yf, k2tog tbl, k3 in A. *60 sts.*

ROW 5: K3 in A, change to MC, k2tog, k1, yf, k2tog tbl, k7, [k2tog, yf, k1, yf, k2tog tbl, k7] x 3 times, k2tog, yf, k1, yf, k2tog tbl, k1, k3 in A. *59 sts.*

WORKING SIMPLE LACE STITCHES

"Lace knitting is made up of a series of increases and decreases to create open-work patterns, in which the working yarn is taken over the needle to make a decorative hole. There are various methods for working yarnovers, but this is the simplest. Known as yarn forward, this method is used when you have just worked a knit stitch or a knit two together decrease and are continuing with another knit stitch after the yarnover."

STEP 1 Following the lace pattern, work to the position of the decrease.

STEP 2 Work the decrease by knitting two stitches together as given in the instructions.

STEP 3 Work the yarn forward by bringing the working yarn to the front of the work between the tips of the two needles.

STEP 4 Take the yarn to the back of the work over the right-hand needle and knit the next stitch as usual.

ROW 7: K3 in A, change to MC, k2tog, k3, k2tog, yf, k1, yf, k2tog tbl, k1, [k6, k2tog, yf, k1, yf, k2tog tbl, k1] x 3 times, k4, k2tog, k3 in A. *57 sts.*

ROW 9: K3 in A, change to MC, k2tog, k1, k2tog, yf, k3, yf, k2tog tbl, [k5, k2tog, yf, k3, yf, k2tog tbl] x 3 times, k5, k3 in A. *56 sts.*

ROW II: K3 in A, change to MC, k2tog, k1, k2tog, yf, k1, yf, k2tog tbl, k1, [k6, k2tog, yf, k1, yf, k2tog tbl, k1] x 3 times, k3, k2tog, k3 in A. *54 sts.*

Break off MC and cont in A only.

Change to 3mm needles.

ROW I: K3, k2tog, k to end of row. *53 sts.*

ROW 2: K to end of row.

ROW 3: K3, k2tog, k to last 5 sts, k2tog, k3. *51 sts.*

WORK PICOT CAST-OFF

NEXT ROW: Cast off 2 sts, * turn, cast on 2 sts using cable cast-on method, turn, pass second st on RH needle over first, pass third st on RH needle over first, cast off 2 sts, rep from * until all sts have been cast off.

ADD TOP PANEL

Using 3mm needles and A, with RS of work facing upwards, pick up and k 61 sts along cast-on edge.

ROW I (WS): K3, p to last 3 sts, k3.

ROW 2: K to end of row.

Work the last two rows a further two times and then rep Row 1 one further time, ending with a WS row.

Cont in twisted stitch pattern.

ROW I: * Skip first st, k into second st, k into first st, let two loops slip off LH needle tog; rep from * to last st, k1.

ROW 2: P to end of row.

Work the last two rows one further time.

ROW I: K1, * skip first st, k into second st, k into first st, let two loops slip off LH needle tog; rep from * to end of row.

ROW 2: P to end of row.

Cast off knitwise and fasten off.

TO MAKE RIGHT SIDE OF COLLAR

Work as given for Left Side, reversing all shaping.

TO MAKE BACK TIES (MAKE TWO)

Here are two different methods for making ties.
Option A has been worked on Colourway 1, whilst Option B has been worked on Colourway 2.

OPTION A

Using 3mm needles and A, cast on 7 sts using the lace cast-on method.

Work 7 sts in twisted stitch pattern as before until ties are 30cm long when slightly stretched. Cast off.

OPTION B

Using 3mm needles and A, cast on 141 sts using the lace cast-on method.

ROW I: * Skip first st, knit into second st, knit into first st, let two loops slip off LH needle tog; rep from * to last st, k1.

ROW 2: P to end of row.

ROW 3: K1, * skip first st, knit into second st, knit into first st, let two loops slip off LH needle tog; rep from * to end of row.

Cast off purlwise and fasten off.

TO MAKE COVERED BUTTON

Here are two different methods for covering buttons.
Option A has been worked on Colourway 1, whilst Option B has been used on Colourway 2.

OPTION A

Using a self-cover button and a piece of your tension swatch cut to slightly larger than the circumference on the button, cover the top surface of the button by catching the raw edges of the knitting and sew them together on the underside of the button. Work a round of buttonhole or blanket stitch around the circumference of the button.

OPTION B

Using either MC or A, work an extra tie. Coil the tie up tightly and stitch to secure. Work a round of buttonhole stitch around the circumference. Embroider several French knots all over the top surface of the button.

TO MAKE UP

Sew a tie at the top centre back edge of each collar piece.
Embroider a row of French Knots in yarn A along any of the twisted stitch rows on each side of the collar.
With right sides facing upwards, lay the two halves of the collar together with the centre fronts slightly overlapping at the top edge.
Sew the button securely in place to join the two halves of the collar at the centre front.

LACE TOP
WITH BOW

learn

SIZE

UK	8	10	12	14	16
TO FIT BUST (CM)	76	81	86	91	97
TO FIT BUST (IN)	30	32	34	36	38
ACTUAL BUST (CM)	81	85	91	95	101
ACTUAL BUST (IN)	32	33½	36	37½	39¾
LENGTH (CM)	47	49	51	53	55
LENGTH (IN)	18½	19¼	20	21	21½

YOU WILL NEED

4-ply weight mohair wool yarn, such as Debbie Bliss
  Angel, in the following colours:
A 2 (2: 2: 2: 2) x 25g balls in off white (Angel, Ivory)
B 1 x 25g ball in mid pink (Angel, Coral)
C 1 x 25g ball in pale pink (Angel, Candyfloss)
Pair each of 4mm and 4.5mm knitting needles
Stitch holder
Tapestry needle
3.25mm crochet hook (optional)

TENSION

20 sts and 32 rows to 10cm square worked over stocking
stitch on 4.5mm needles. Adjust needle size as necessary
to obtain tension.

ABBREVIATIONS

See standard abbreviations on page 7.

TO MAKE THE BACK

Using 4mm needles and A, cast on 81 (85: 91: 95: 101) sts.
ROW I (RS): K to end.
ROW 2: P to end.
These two rows form the stocking stitch (st st) pattern.
Cont to work in st st but AT THE SAME TIME dec 1 st at
each end of every 4th (4th: 5th: 5th: 5th) row until there
are 67 (71: 77: 81: 87) sts, changing to 4.5mm needles
after 32 rows have been worked.
Cont to work in st st without shaping for a further 20 (22:
16: 18: 19) rows.
Cont to work in st st but AT THE SAME TIME inc 1 st at
each end of every 5th (5th: 5th: 5th: 6th) row until there
are 81 (85: 91: 95: 101) sts.
Cont to work in st st without shaping for a further 7 (9:
10: 10: 6) rows, ending with a WS row.

SHAPE ARMHOLES

Cast off 2 (2: 3: 3: 4) sts at beg of next 2 rows. *77 (81: 85:
89: 93) sts.*
Dec 1 st at each end of next 2 (3: 4: 5: 6) rows, then 2 (1:
1: 1: –) foll alt rows, then 1 (2: 1: 1: 1) foll 4th (3rd: 3rd:
5th: 3rd) rows, and then foll – (–: 5th: –: 5th) row. *67 (69:
71: 75: 77) sts.*
**
Cont to work in st st without shaping until Back measures
18.5 (19.5: 20.5: 21.5: 22.5)cm from beg of armhole
shaping, ending with a WS row.

SHAPE BACK NECK AND SHOULDERS

NEXT ROW (RS): K 18 (19: 20: 22: 23) sts, turn, leave rem
sts on a stitch holder.
Work each side of neck separately.
NEXT ROW: P3, p2tog, p to end of row. *17 (18: 19: 21: 22) sts.*
NEXT ROW (RS): Cast off 5 (5: 5: 6: 6) sts, knit to last 5
sts, k2tog, k3. *11 (12: 13: 14: 15) sts.*
NEXT ROW: P to end of row.
NEXT ROW: Cast off 5 (5: 6: 6: 7) sts, knit to last 5 sts,
k2tog, k3. *5 (6: 6: 7: 7) sts.*

NEXT ROW: P to end of row.

Cast off rem 5 (6: 6: 7: 7) sts.

With RS facing, rejoin A to rem sts.

NEXT ROW: Cast off centre 31 sts, k to end of row.

NOTE: Take care not to cast off centre stitches too tightly as sides of neck will pull inwards.

Complete neck and shoulders to match first side, reversing all shaping.

QUATREFOIL LACE PATTERN (QF) USED ON FRONT (10-ROW REPEAT WORKED OVER 15 STS)

NOTE: As lace stitches are increased and decreased over the 10-row repeat lace pattern, do not count sts within this panel on the 6th, 7th, 8th or 9th rows.

ROW 1 (RS): K5, k2tog, yf, k1, yf, sl1, k1, psso, k5.

ROW 2: P4, p2tog tbl, yrn, p3, yrn, p2tog, p4.

ROW 3: K3, k2tog, yf, k5, yf, sl 1, k1, psso, k3.

ROW 4: P2, p2tog tbl, yrn, p1, yrn, p2tog, p1, p2tog tbl, yrn, p1, yrn, p2tog, p2.

ROW 5: K1, k2tog, yf, k3, yf, k3tog, yf, k3, yf, sl 1, k1, psso, k1.

ROW 6: P2, yrn, p5, yrn, p1, yrn, p5, yrn, p2.

ROW 7: [K3, yf, sl1, k1, psso, k1, k2tog, yf] twice, k3.

ROW 8: P4, p3tog, yrn, p5, yrn, p3tog, p4.

ROW 9: K6, yf, sl1, k1, psso, k1, k2tog, yf, k6.

ROW 10: P3, p2tog tbl, p2, yrn, p3tog, yrn, p2, p2tog, p3.

FANCY SHELL LACE PATTERN (FS) USED ON FRONT (4-ROW REPEAT WORKED OVER 9STS)

ROW 1 (RS): P2, k1, [yo, k1] 4 times, p2.

ROW 2: K2, p1, [k1, p1] 4 times, k2.

ROW 3: P2, k1, p1, ssk, k1, k2tog, p1, k1, p2.

ROW 4: K2, p1, k1, p3tog, k1, p1, k2.

TO MAKE FRONT

Using 4mm needles and A, cast on 81 (85: 91: 95: 101) sts.

ROW 1 (RS): K 20 (22: 25: 27: 30) in A, work 9 sts of Row 1 of FS patt in B, k4 in A, work 15 sts of Row 1 of QF patt in C, k4 in A, work 9 sts of Row 1 of FS patt in B, k 20 (22: 25: 27: 30) in A.

NOTE: Link yarns when changing colour along a row using the intarsia method to avoid a hole (see instructions give on page 90).

This last row sets the position of the lace panels.

Cont to work in st st with inset lace panels in contrast colours as set but AT THE SAME TIME work as given for Back until **. *67 (69: 71: 75: 77) sts.*

Cont to work in st st without shaping keeping inset lace

panels correct as set until work measures 9 (10: 11: 12: 13) cm from beg of armhole shaping, ending with a WS row.

SHAPE FRONT NECK

NEXT ROW (RS): K 13 (14: 15: 17: 18) in A, work 9 sts of FS patt in B, k4 in A, work first 3 sts of QF patt in C, turn and leave rem sts on a stitch holder.

Work each side of neck separately.

NEXT ROW (WS): Cast off 4 sts purlwise in C, p3 in A, work 9 sts of FS patt in B, p to end in A. *25 (26: 27: 29: 30) sts.*

NOTE: Do not cast off centre stitches too tightly as sides of the neck will pull inwards.

Dec 1 st at neck edge of next 7 rows, then foll alt row, then foll 6th row, then foll 10th row. *15 (16: 17: 19: 20) sts.* Cont to work in patt as set without shaping for a further 5 rows, ending with a WS row.

SHAPE SHOULDER

NEXT ROW (RS): Cast off 5 (5: 5: 6: 6) sts, patt to end of row. *10 (11: 12: 13: 14) sts.*

NEXT ROW (WS): Patt to end of row.

NEXT ROW (RS): Cast off 5 (5: 6: 6: 7) sts, patt to end of row. *5 (6: 6: 7: 7) sts.*

NEXT ROW (WS): Patt to end of row.

Cast off rem 5 (6: 6: 7: 7) sts.

With RS facing, rejoin C to rem sts.

NEXT ROW: Cast off centre 9 sts, patt to end of row.

NOTE: Do not cast off centre stitches too tightly as sides of the neck will pull inwards.

Complete to match first side of neck, reversing all shaping.

TO MAKE NECK TIE

Using 4mm needles and B, cast on 9 sts.

ROW 1: K2, [p1, k1] three times, k1.

ROW 2: K1, [p1, k1] four times.

Repeat last two rows until Neck Tie measures 140cm.

Cast off.

TO MAKE UP

Join shoulder seams. Join side seams using mattress stitch. Place centre of one side edge of Neck Tie at centre back of neck, sew in position all round neck edge to outer edges of QF lace panel, leaving front bands free to tie in a bow.

ADD PICOT EDGES (OPTIONAL)

Using 3.25mm crochet hook and A, pick up and work as folls along lower edge of top either into each stitch or into stitch loops between sts: make 3 chain, 1 single crochet. Repeat using C around both armhole edges.

"THIS LACE TOP IS PERFECT FOR ALL SEASONS and can be dressed up or down. Wear it on its own in summer, whilst in winter pair it with a cardigan or jacket. Once you have mastered both lace knitting and intarsia techniques in this lightweight fabric, you too will want to jump for joy!"

RANDOM STRIPED
SWEATER

 *learn*

SIZE

UK	8	10	12	14	16
TO FIT BUST (CM)	81	86	91	97	102
TO FIT BUST (IN)	32	34	36	38	40
ACTUAL BUST (CM)	83	88	93	98	103
ACTUAL BUST (IN)	32½	34½	36½	38½	40½
LENGTH (CM)	47	49.5	52	55.5	57.5
LENGTH (IN)	18½	19½	20½	21½	22½
SLEEVE SEAM (CM)	45.5	46	46	47.5	47.5
SLEEVE SEAM (IN)	18	18¼	18¼	18¾	18¾

YOU WILL NEED

Double-knitting weight wool yarn, such as BC-Garn
  Semilla Organic DK, in the following colours:

FOR COLOURWAY ONE
A 3 (4: 5: 5: 6) x 50g balls in mid blue (Teal)
B 1 x 50g ball in mustard (Relish)
C 1 x 50g ball in pale blue (Duck Egg Blue)
D 1 x 50g ball in pale purple (Wysteria)
E 1 x 50g ball in mid brown (Truffle Brown)
F 1 x 50g ball in deep pink (Rose)
G 1 x 50g ball in dark grey (Charcoal Grey)
H 1 x 50g ball in deep red (Plum Wine)
I 1 x 50g ball in mid purple (Lavender)
J 1 x 50g ball in turquoise (Turquoise)

FOR COLOURWAY TWO
A 3 (4: 5: 5: 6) x 50g balls in lilac (Dusty Lilac)
B 1 x 50g ball in mauve (Mauve)
C 1 x 50g ball in pale grey (Light Grey)
D 1 x 50g ball in turquoise (Turquoise)
E 1 x 50g ball in mid green (Grass)
F 1 x 50g ball in deep pink (Rose)
G 1 x 50g ball in mid brown (Truffle Brown)
H 1 x 50g ball in deep purple (Deep Purple)
I 1 x 50g ball in bright purple (Bright Purple)
J 1 x 50g ball in pale purple (Wysteria)

Pair each of size 3.75mm and 4mm knitting needles
3.75mm circular knitting needle
Stitch holder
Tapestry needle

TENSION

24 sts and 36 rows to 10cm square worked over stocking
stitch on 4mm needles. Adjust needle size as necessary to
obtain tension.

ABBREVIATIONS

See standard abbreviations on page 9.

STRIPE SEQUENCE FOR COLOURWAY ONE

**

F	3 rows		E	3 rows
G	1 row		F	1 row
D	2 rows		G	2 rows
J	4 rows		I	3 rows
H	2 rows		B	2 rows
B	1 row		H	1 row
A	3 rows		A	3 rows
C	1 row		G	3 rows
D	1 row		C	2 rows
E	2 rows		B	1 row
G	3 rows		D	2 rows
F	2 rows		E	2 rows
J	1 row		J	1 row
B	2 rows		H	2 rows
H	1 row		C	1 row
I	3 rows		F	2 rows
G	1 row		B	3 rows
C	2 rows		G	2 rows
E	3 rows		J	3 rows
F	2 rows		I	2 rows
B	3 rows		H	1 row
A	2 rows		E	1 row
H	1 row		A	2 rows
D	3 rows		B	1 row
G	2 rows		D	3 rows
J	3 rows		A	1 row
E	2 rows		F	2 rows
B	2 rows		C	3 rows
C	1 row		E	3 rows
H	2 rows		H	2 rows
I	1 row		B	3 rows
G	1 row		G	1 row
A	2 rows		J	2 rows
D	1 row		F	1 row
F	4 rows		I	3 rows
C	2 rows		H	1 row
J	3 rows		C	2 rows
D	2 rows		A	4 rows

repeat from **

STRIPE SEQUENCE FOR COLOURWAY TWO

**

F	3 rows		F	2 rows
D	2 rows		I	2 rows
E	1 row		E	2 rows
C	3 rows		C	3 rows
G	2 rows		H	1 row
B	2 rows		J	1 row
E	2 rows		G	4 rows
A	3 rows		B	2 rows
H	2 rows		E	1 row
F	1 row		D	3 rows
I	3 rows		H	2 rows
C	4 rows		A	3 rows
J	2 rows		I	4 rows
D	3 rows		G	2 rows
H	1 row		J	3 rows
B	3 rows		F	3 rows
F	2 rows		C	4 rows
I	1 row		B	3 rows
G	2 rows		H	1 row
E	3 rows		J	1 row
A	4 rows		E	2 rows
H	2 rows		A	2 rows
J	3 rows		I	3 rows
C	4 rows		H	1 row
D	2 rows		F	1 row
I	1 row		G	2 rows
A	2 rows		D	3 rows
F	3 rows		B	2 rows
G	2 rows		E	1 row
H	1 row		J	3 rows
E	2 rows		F	2 rows
B	3 rows		H	2 rows
A	1 row		C	3 rows
J	3 rows		I	3 rows

repeat from **

TO MAKE THE BACK

Using 3.75mm needles and B, cast on 82 (88: 94: 100: 106) sts.

ROW 1 (RS): * K1, p1; rep from * to end of row.

ROW 2: * K1, p1; rep from * to end of row.

The last two rows form the single rib (k1, p1 rib) pattern.

Cont to work in single rib as set for a further 12 rows, ending with a WS row.

Change to 4mm needles and F.

ROW 1 (INC): K3, m1, knit to last 3 sts, m1, k3.

ROW 2: P to end of row.

Cont to work in stocking stitch (st st) without shaping for a further 8 rows.

Cont to work in st st but inc 1 st at each end of next and every 10th row as set but AT THE SAME TIME foll stripe sequence until 90 (100: 108: 118: 126) rows have been worked. *100 (106: 112: 118: 124) sts.*

SHAPE ARMHOLES

Keeping stripe sequence correct, cast off 4 (4: 4: 6: 6) sts at beg of next 2 rows. *92 (98: 104: 106: 112) sts.*

NEXT ROW: K1, skpo, k to last 3 sts, k2tog, k1.

NEXT ROW: P to end of row.

Rep last two rows until 58 (64: 70: 70: 76) sts rem.
**

Keeping stripe sequence correct, cont to work in st st without shaping for a further 24 rows.

NEXT ROW (RS): K12 (15: 18: 18: 21), k2tog, turn, leave rem unworked sts on a stitch holder.

NEXT ROW: K2tog, p to end of row.

NEXT ROW (RS): Cast off 6 (7: 9: 9: 10) sts at shoulder edge.

NEXT ROW: P to end of row.

Cast off rem 6 (8: 9: 9: 11) sts.

Leaving centre 30 sts on a stitch holder, with RS facing rejoin yarn at neck edge.

NEXT ROW (RS): K2tog, k to end.

NEXT ROW: P to last 2 sts, k2tog.

NEXT ROW: K to end of row.

NEXT ROW: Cast off 6 (7: 9: 9: 10) sts, p to end of row.

Cast off rem 6 (8: 9: 9: 11) sts.

TO MAKE THE FRONT

Work as given for Back until ******.

Work each side of neck separately.

ROW 1 (RS): K17 (20: 23: 23: 26), k2tog, turn, leave rem unworked sts on a stitch holder.

ROW 2: P to end of row.

Rep last two rows until 12 (15: 18: 18: 21) sts rem.

Keeping stripe sequence correct, cont to work in st st without shaping for a further 12 rows.

NEXT ROW: Cast off 6 (7: 9: 9: 10) sts.

NEXT ROW: P to end of row.

Cast off rem 6 (8: 9: 9: 11) sts.

Leaving centre 20 sts on a stitch holder, with RS facing rejoin yarn at neck edge.

Complete right side of neck to match left side, reversing all shaping.

TO MAKE THE SLEEVES (MAKE TWO)

Using size 3.75mm needles and B, cast on 48 (54: 60: 66: 72) sts.

ROW 1 (RS): * K1, p1; rep from * to end of row.

ROW 2: * K1, p1; rep from * to end of row.

The last two rows form the single rib (k1, p1 rib) pattern.

Cont to work in single rib as set for a further 12 rows, ending with a WS row.

Change to 4mm needles and A.

Cont to work in st st but AT THE SAME TIME inc 1 st at each end of next and every 10th row until 74 (80: 86: 92: 98) sts.

Cont to work in st st without shaping until Sleeve measures 45 (46: 47: 48: 49)cm from cast-on edge.

Cast off 4 (4: 4: 6: 6) sts at beg of next 2 rows. *66 (72: 78: 80: 86) sts.*

NEXT ROW: K1, skpo, k to last 3 sts, k2tog, k1.

Cont to work in st st without shaping for a further 3 rows.

Rep last four rows a further 9 times. *46 (52: 58: 60: 66) sts.*

NEXT ROW: K1, skpo, k to last 3 sts, k2tog, k1.

NEXT ROW: K to end of row.

Rep last two rows until 36 (42: 48: 50: 56) sts rem.

Cast off 3 sts at beg of next 6 rows.

Cast off rem 18 (24: 30: 32: 38) sts.

TO MAKE UP

Weave in any loose yarn ends.

Join the shoulder seams using backstitch.

Using 3.75mm circular needle and B, with RS facing and starting at left shoulder seam, pick up 24 sts down left front neck, 20 sts from stitch holder at centre front neck, 24 sts up right front neck to right shoulder seam, 5 sts down back right neck, 30 sts from stitch holder at centre back neck and 45 sts up back left neck. *108 sts.*

Working in rounds, work 6 rounds in single rib (k1, p1 rib).

Cast off loosely in rib.

COLLEGE-STYLE CARDIGAN
WITH PATCH POCKET

"WITH ITS SHORT AND SNUGGLY FITTED SHAPE, worked in tweedy Shetland yarn with tiny buttons running up the front, this preppy, college-style cardigan brings together the worlds of traditional British handknitting and American varsity jackets. This cardigan is partly knitted in a simple twist stitch, which gives the fabric a really lovely texture."

SIZE

UK	8	10	12	14	16
TO FIT BUST (CM)	81	86	91	97	102
TO FIT BUST (IN)	32	34	36	38	40
ACTUAL BUST (CM)	81	86	91	97	102
ACTUAL BUST (IN)	32	34	36	38	40
LENGTH (CM)	42	43.5	45	47	48.5
LENGTH (IN)	16½	17	17¾	18½	19
SLEEVE SEAM (CM)	44	44.5	45	45.5	46
SLEEVE SEAM (IN)	17¼	17½	17¾	18	18¼

YOU WILL NEED

4-ply wool yarn, such as Jamieson's Spindrift, in the following colours:
A   3 (4: 5: 6: 7) x 25g balls in red (Spindrift, Poppy)
B   5 (6: 7: 8: 9) x 25g balls in beige (Spindrift, Eesit)
Pair each of size 2.75mm and 3.25mm knitting needles
Two large safety pins
10 small buttons, 1.5cm in diameter
Tapestry needle

TENSION

24 sts and 34 rows to 10cm square worked over stocking stitch on 3.25mm needles. Adjust needle size as necessary to obtain tension.

ABBREVIATIONS

TWIST 2 Ignore first stitch, knit into second stitch, knit into first stitch, drop both stitches off the needle together (see instructions given on page 86 for working this twist stitch pattern).
See also standard abbreviations on page 9.

PATTERN NOTES

Twist stitch pattern is always worked in A, while stocking stitch pattern is always worked in B. Link yarns when changing colour to avoid a hole.

TO MAKE THE BACK

Using 2.75mm needles and B, cast on 91 (97: 103: 109: 115) sts.

ROW 1 (RS): * K2, p2; rep from * to last 3 (1: 3: 1: 3) sts, k 2 (1: 2: 1: 2), p 1 (–: 1: –: 1).

ROW 2: K 1 (–: 1: –: 1), p 2 (1: 2: 1: 2), * k2, p2; rep from * to end of row.

These two rows form the double rib (k2, p2 rib) pattern. Cont to work in double rib for a further 12 rows, ending with a WS row.

Change to 3.25mm needles and A, then cont as folls:

ROW 1 (RS): K1, * twist 2, k1; rep from * to end of row.

ROW 2: P to end of row.

These two rows form the twist stitch pattern. Cont to work in twist stitch for a further 22 rows, ending with a WS row.

SHAPE SIDES

Cont to work in twist stitch but AT THE SAME TIME inc 1 st at each end of next and every foll 18th (18th: 19th: 20th: 20th) row, taking inc sts into patt, until there are 97 (103: 109: 115: 121) sts.

Cont to work in twist stitch without shaping until Back measures 22 (22.5: 23: 24: 24.5)cm from cast-on edge, ending with a WS row.

Using B, work 4 rows in stocking stitch (st st).

Using A, work 6 rows in twist stitch.

SHAPE ARMHOLES

Using B only, cont to work in st st but AT THE SAME TIME shape armholes as folls:

Cast off 4 (5: 5: 6: 6) sts at beg of next 2 rows.

Dec 1 st at each end of next 4 (5: 5: 6: 6) rows and then 2 (2: 3: 3: 4) foll alt rows. *77 (79: 83: 85: 89) sts.*

Cont to work in st st without shaping until Back measures 42 (43.5: 45: 47: 48.5)cm from cast-on edge, ending with a WS row.

SHAPE SHOULDERS AND BACK NECK

NEXT ROW (RS): Cast off 6 (7: 7: 8: 8) sts, k until there are 17 (17: 19: 19: 21) sts on RH needle, turn, leave rem unworked sts on a stitch holder.

Work each side of neck separately.

Cast off 2 sts at beg of next row, cast off 7 (7: 8: 8: 9) sts at beg of foll row, then dec 1 st at beg of foll row.

Cast off rem 7 (7: 8: 8: 9) sts.

With RS facing, rejoin A to rem sts from stitch holder.

NEXT ROW (RS): Cast off centre 31 sts, k to end of row.

NEXT ROW (WS): Cast off 6 (7: 7: 8: 8) sts, p to end of row.

17 (17: 19: 19: 21) sts.

Complete to match first side of neck, reversing all shaping.

TO MAKE LEFT FRONT

Using 2.75mm needles and B, cast on 49 (52: 55: 58: 61) sts.

ROW 1 (RS): P1, k2 (k2: k1: –: p1, k2), * p2, k2; rep from * to last 6 sts, [k1, p1] 3 times.

ROW 2: [P1, k1] 3 times, * p2, k2; rep from * to last 3 (2: 1: –: 3) sts, p2, k1 (p2: p1: –: p2, k1).

These two rows form the double rib (k2, p2 rib) pattern with a 6 moss-stitch band at front edge.

Cont to work in double rib with moss-stitch band as set for a further 11 rows, ending with a RS row.

NEXT ROW (WS): Work 6 sts in moss st and slip onto a safety pin, rib to end of row. *43 (46: 49: 52: 55) sts on needle.*

Change to 3.25mm needles and A, then cont as folls:

ROW 1 (RS): K1, * twist 2, k1; rep from * to end of row.

ROW 2: P to end of row.

These two rows form the twist stitch pattern.

Cont to work in twist stitch for a further 22 rows, ending with a WS row.

SHAPE SIDES

Cont to work in twist stitch but AT THE SAME TIME inc 1 st at side edge of next and every foll 18th (18th: 19th: 20th: 20th) row, taking inc sts into patt, until there are 46 (49: 52: 55: 58) sts.

Cont to work in twist stitch without shaping until Left Front matches Back to beg of armhole shaping, ending with a WS row.

SHAPE ARMHOLE

Cont to work in twist stitch but AT THE SAME TIME shape armholes as folls:

Cast off 4 (5: 5: 6: 6) sts at beg of next row.

Work 1 row.

Dec 1 st at armhole edge of next 4 (5: 5: 6: 6) rows and then 2 (2: 3: 3: 4) foll alt rows. *36 (37: 39: 40: 42) sts.*

Cont to work in twist stitch without shaping for a further 5 (7: 5: 7: 7) rows, ending with a RS (WS: WS: RS: RS) row.

Cont to work without shaping but AT THE SAME TIME work the diagonal shoulder stripes using A and B, maintaining the vertical continuity of the twist stitch in the main panel, as folls:

ROW 1: Using B work 1 st in st st at armhole edge – so for this Row 1 it is the last (first: first: last: last) st – then using A work remainder of row in twist stitch.

Work an additional 1 st in st st using B at armhole edge

than on the preceding row on next 3 rows until 4 sts are worked in B at armhole edge.

NOTE: The overall number of stitches remains the same but more B sts and fewer A sts are worked on each row.

ROW 5: Using A work 1 st in twist st at armhole edge, then using B work 4 sts in st st, then using A work remainder of row in twist stitch.

Work an additional 1 st in twist st using A at armhole edge than on the preceding row on next 5 rows until 6 sts are worked in A at armhole edge.

NOTE: The overall number of stitches remains the same but the 4-st stripe worked in B moves position on each row towards the front edge.

ROW 11: Using B work 1 st in st st at armhole edge, then using A work 6 sts in twist st, then using B work 4 sts in st st, then using A work remainder of row in twist stitch.

Work an additional 1 st in st st using B at armhole edge than on preceding row, adjusting the position of both A and B stripes on all subsequent rows, until 10 sts are worked in A at front edge, ending with a RS row.

SHAPE NECK

Cont to work in patt as set, adjusting position of stripes on each subsequent row, but AT THE SAME TIME shape neck as folls:

NEXT ROW (WS): Cast off 6 sts, patt to end of row.
NEXT ROW: Patt to end of row.
NEXT ROW (WS): Cast off 3 sts, patt to end of row.
NEXT ROW: Patt to end of row.
NEXT ROW (WS): Cast off 2 sts, patt to end of row.
NEXT ROW: Patt to end of row.

Cont to work in patt as set but AT THE SAME TIME dec 1 st at neck edge of next 3 rows, and then 2 foll 4th rows. *20 (21: 23: 24: 26) sts.*

NOTE: During the neck shaping the stripes will reach the front neck edge, at which point work in st st using B only. Cont to work in st st without shaping until Left Front measures same as Back to start of shoulder shaping, ending with a WS row.

SHAPE SHOULDERS

Cast off 6 (7: 7: 8: 8) sts at beg of next row.
Work 1 row.
Cast off 7 (7: 8: 8: 9) sts at beg of next row.
Work 1 row.
Cast off rem 7 (7: 8: 8: 9) sts.

TO MAKE RIGHT FRONT

Using 2.75mm needles and B, cast on 49 (52: 55: 58: 61) sts.
ROW 1 (RS): [K1, p1] 3 times, * k2, p2; rep from * to last 3 (2: 1: –: 3) sts, k2, p1 (k2: k1: –: k2, p1).
ROW 2 (WS): K1, p2 (p2: p1: –: k1, p2), * k2, p2; rep from * to last 6 sts, [p1, k1] 3 times.
These two rows form the double rib (k2, p2 rib) pattern with a 6 moss-stitch band at front edge.
Cont to work in double rib with moss-stitch band as set for a further 2 rows, ending with a WS row.
BUTTONHOLE ROW (RS): Work 3 sts in moss st, yrn, k2tog, patt to end of row.
Cont to work in double rib with moss-stitch band as set for a further 7 rows, ending with a WS row.
NEXT ROW (RS): Work 6 sts in moss st and slip onto a safety pin, rib to end of row. *43 (46: 49: 52: 55) sts on needle.* Work 1 further double rib row.
Change to 3.25mm needles and A, then cont to work as given for Left Front, reversing all shaping.

TO MAKE SLEEVE (MAKE TWO)

Using 2.75mm needles and A, cast on 51 (53: 55: 57: 59) sts.
Work in double rib (k2, p2 rib) as given for Back but AT THE SAME TIME inc 1 st at each end of 6th (6th: 6th: 5th: 5th) row and every foll 6th (6th: 6th: 5th: 5th) row until there are 59 (61: 63: 67: 69) sts.
Cont to work in double rib until Sleeve measures 8cm from cast-on edge, ending with a WS row.
Change to 3.25mm needles and B, then work 4 rows in st st.
Change to A, then cont as folls:

FOR 1ST SIZE ONLY
ROW 1 (RS): K2, twist 2, * k1, twist 2; rep from * to last st, k1.
ROW 2: P to end of row.

FOR 2ND AND 4TH SIZES ONLY
ROW 1 (RS): * K1, twist 2; rep from * to last st, k1.
ROW 2: P to end of row.

FOR 3RD AND 5TH SIZES ONLY
ROW 1 (RS): * K1, twist 2; rep from * to end of row.
ROW 2: P to end of row.

These two rows form the twist stitch pattern.
Cont to work in twist stitch for a further 4 rows, ending with a WS row.
Change to B, then cont to work 2 (2: 3: 3: 3) rows in st st.

WORKING THE TWIST STITCH

"The red sections of this garment are mostly knitted using a simple twist stitch, which is a 3-stitch repeat pattern. The twist stitch is based on the same principle as any cable stitch, however, as the twists are so small – with only two stitches to each twist – this technique can be executed without the use of a cable needle."

STEP I The first stitch in the 3-stitch repeat pattern is knitted as usual, while the next 2 stitches are twisted. For 'twist 2', work as follows: ignoring the first stitch on the left-hand needle, insert the right-hand needle up into the second stitch on the left needle.

STEP 2 Wrap the yarn round the needle from back to front and pull the yarn through the stitch with the right-hand needle, but do not slide the stitch off the left-hand needle yet as you would if you were knitting the stitch normally.

STEP 3 With the new loop still on the right-hand needle, knit into the first stitch on the left-hand needle previously ignored. Wrap the yarn round the needle from back to front and bring through to create another loop on your right-hand needle.

STEP 4 With these two new loops on the right-hand needle, gently slide both of the stitches that you have just knitted off the left-hand needle.

SHAPE SIDES

Cont to work in st st but AT THE SAME TIME inc 1 st at each end of next and every foll 13th row until there are 77 (79: 81: 85: 87) sts.

Cont to work in st st without shaping until Sleeve measures 44 (44.5: 45: 45.5: 46)cm from cast-on edge, ending with a WS row.

SHAPE SLEEVEHEAD

Cast off 4 sts at beg of next 2 rows. *69 (71: 73: 77: 79) sts.*

Dec 1 st at each end of next 4 rows, then on 4 foll alt rows, then on foll 4th row.

Dec 1 st at each end of foll 8th (9th: 10th: 12th: 14th) row, foll 7th (9th: 10th: 12th: 14th) row, then foll 4th row.

Dec 1 st at each end of 3 (2: 1: 1: –) foll alt rows, then next 5 (8: 10: 8: 10) rows.

FOR 4TH AND 5TH SIZES ONLY

Cast off 4 sts at beg of next 2 rows.

ALL SIZES

Cast off rem 29 (27: 27: 27: 27) sts.

TO MAKE PATCH POCKET

Using 3.25mm needles and B, cast on 20 sts.

Work in st st until Pocket measures 7cm from cast-on edge, ending with a WS row.

Change to 2.75mm needles and work in double rib (k2, p2 rib) as given for Back until work measures 8.5cm from cast-on edge.

Cast off in rib.

TO MAKE UP

Join shoulder seams using backstitch.

WORK BUTTONBAND

With RS facing, slip 6 sts from Left Front safety pin onto 2.75mm needles and rejoin yarn B.

Cont to work in moss st as set until buttonband stretches up Left Front to neck shaping, ending with a WS row.

Place 6 sts on a safety pin.

Slip stitch buttonband in place.

Mark position of 10 buttons on Left Front buttonband. The lowest button must correspond to buttonhole already worked in Right Front buttonhole band. The highest button will sit just above the neck shaping within the neckband that is yet to be worked. Evenly space the remaining 8 buttons between these two.

WORK BUTTONHOLE BAND

With WS facing, slip 6 sts from Right Front safety pin onto 2.75mm needles and rejoin yarn B.

Cont to work in moss st as set until buttonhole band stretches up Right Front to neck shaping, ending with a WS row, but AT THE SAME TIME work 8 buttonholes to correspond with the marked positions on the buttonband as folls:

BUTTONHOLE ROW (RS): Work 3 sts in moss st, yrn, k2tog, moss st to end of row.

Place 6 sts on a safety pin.

Slip stitch buttonhole band in place.

WORK NECKBAND

With RS facing and B, pick up and moss st 6 sts from safety pin of buttonhole band sts, 44 (45: 45: 48: 48) sts up right side of neck, 40 (42: 42: 44: 44) sts across Back neck, 44 (45: 45: 48: 48) sts down left side of neck, then 6 sts from safety pin of buttonband. *140 (144: 144: 152: 152)* sts.

Con to work in moss st as set for 3 rows.

BUTTONHOLE ROW (RS): Work 3 sts in moss st, yrn, k2tog, moss st to end of row.

Cont to work in moss st as set for 4 further rows, ending with a RS row.

Cast off in moss st.

TO FINISH

Set in the sleeves, matching the centre points of the sleeveheads to the shoulder seams.

Join the side and sleeve seams.

Slip stitch the patch pocket in place on the Left Front.

Sew the buttons securely onto the Left Front buttonband to correspond with Right Front buttonholes.

SHAWL COLLAR CARDIGAN
WITH FLORAL EMBROIDERY

SIZE

UK	6	8	10	12	14
TO FIT BUST (CM)	76	81	86	91	97
TO FIT BUST (IN)	30	32	34	36	38
ACTUAL BUST (CM)	77	81	87	91	97
ACTUAL BUST (IN)	30¼	32	34¼	36	38
LENGTH (CM)	47.5	49	50	51.5	53.5
LENGTH (IN)	18¾	19¼	19¾	20¼	21
SLEEVE SEAM (CM)	44	44.5	45	45.5	46
SLEEVE SEAM (IN)	17¼	17½	17¾	18	18¼

YOU WILL NEED

Any double-knitting weight wool yarn, such as Blue Sky Alpaca Melange or Blue Sky Alpaca Sport Weight, in the following colours:

MC 8 (9: 10: 11: 12) x 50g hanks in mid blue (Melange, Cornflower)

A 1 x 50g hank in mustard (Melange, Dijon)

B 1 x 50g hank in bright pink (Sport Weight, Hibiscus)

Oddments of tapestry wool or similar wool yarn, such as Laine St Pierre Darning Wool, in the following colours:

C gold (Mustard)

D off white (Almond)

E dark red (Garnet)

F mauve (Violet)

G dusky pink (Dusky Pink)

H dark blue (Petrol)

I bright green (Pistachio)

Pair each of size 3mm and 3.75mm knitting needles

5 buttons

Tapestry needle

TENSION

20 sts and 30 rows to 10cm square worked over stocking stitch on 3.75mm needles. Adjust needle size as necessary to obtain tension.

ABBREVIATIONS

See standard abbreviations on page 7.

PATTERN NOTE

The floral motif on the Left and Right Fronts can be worked either integrally into the knitting using the intarisa method (see page 90) or embroidered onto the surface of the finished piece using duplicate stitch (see page 129).

TO MAKE THE BACK

Using 3.75mm needles and MC, cast on 73 (77: 83: 87: 93) sts.

ROW 1 (RS): * K2, p2; rep from * to last st, k1.

ROW 2: P1, * k2, p2; rep from * to end of row.

These two rows form the double rib (k2, p2 rib) pattern.

Cont to work in double rib for a further 12 rows.

Change to 3mm needles.

Cont to work in double rib for a further 16 rows, inc 4 sts evenly across the last row. *77 (81: 87: 91: 97) sts.*

Change to 3.75mm needles.

ROW 1 (RS): K to end of row.

ROW 2: P to end of row.

These two rows form the stocking stitch (st st) pattern.

Cont to work in st st until Back measures 27.5 (28: 28: 28.5: 29.5)cm, ending with a WS row, but AT THE SAME TIME inc 1 st at each end of 3rd and every foll 24th (16th: 24th: 16th: 18th) row until there are 81 (87: 91: 97: 103) sts.

SHAPE ARMHOLES

Cast off 5 (5: 5: 6: 7) sts at beg of next 2 rows. *71 (77: 81: 85: 89) sts.*

Dec 1 st at each end of next 3 (3: 3: 3: 5) rows. *65 (71: 75: 79: 79) sts.*

Dec 1 st at each end of foll 1 (2: 3: 3: 2) alt rows. *63 (67: 69: 73: 75) sts.*

Cont to work in st st without shaping until Back measures 47.5 (49: 50: 51.5: 53.5)cm from cast-on edge, ending with a WS row.

MAKING BOBBINS OF YARN AND WORKING MOTIFS IN INTARSIA

"When working in motifs in colour, it is advisable to wind the different colour yarns into separate small bobbins. If you work with whole balls, the yarns will twist together and you will inevitably spend lots of your knitting time untangling threads. Bobbins are easily made by hand. With these made, you can then go on to work blocks or motifs in colour within your knitting, using the intarsia method whereby the different colour yarns are link with a simple twist."

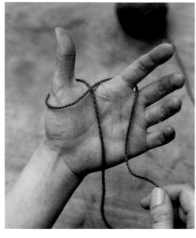

STEP 1 With the tail end of the yarn in the palm of your hand, wrap the yarn in a figure of eight around your thumb and either your forefinger or little finger. The tail end of the yarn will be joined into your work and will be knitted from it this way.

STEP 2 Continue wrapping the yarn into a figure of eight between your thumb and fingers until you have a large enough bobbin to complete the colour area you are going to knit.

STEP 3 Once large enough, slide the yarn off your hand and break the yarn. Wrap the end tightly around the centre of the bobbin to secure it and tuck in the end. Pull gently on the tail end in the centre of the bobbin to ensure the yarn runs smoothly.

STEP 4 To change colour on a knit row, lay the new colour over the existing colour and between the two needles, with the tail end to the left. Bring the new colour under and then over the existing colour. Knit the stitch with the new colour.

STEP 5 Go back and pull gently on the tail end to tighten up the first stitch in the new colour after you have worked a few more stitches.

SHAPE SHOULDERS AND BACK NECK

NEXT ROW (RS): Cast off 5 (6: 6: 6: 7) sts, k until there are 14 (14: 15: 16: 16) sts on RH needle, turn, leave rem unworked sts on a stitch holder.

Work each side of the neck separately.

Cast off 2 sts at beg of next row. *12 (12: 13: 14: 14) sts.*

Cast off 5 (6: 6: 7: 6) sts at beg of next row. *7 (6: 7: 7: 8) sts.*

Dec 1 st at beg of next row. *6 (5: 6: 6: 7) sts.*

Cast off rem 6 (5: 6: 6: 7) sts.

With RS facing, rejoin yarn MC to rem sts.

NEXT ROW (RS): Cast off centre 25 (27: 27: 29: 29) sts, k to end of row.

NEXT ROW: Cast off 5 (6: 6: 6: 7) sts, p to end of row. *14 (14: 15: 16: 16) sts.*

Complete to match first side of neck, reversing all shaping.

TO MAKE LEFT FRONT

Using 3.75mm and MC, cast on 40 (42: 45: 47: 50) sts.

ROW I (RS): K 0 (0: 1: 0: 0), p 2 (0: 2: 1: 0), * k2, p2; rep from * to last 2 sts, k2.

The last row forms the double rib.

Cont to work in double rib as set for a further 13 rows.

Change to 3mm needles.

Cont to work in double rib as set for a further 15 rows.

NEXT ROW (WS): P2, k2, p2, place sts just worked on a stitch holder or safety pin, k2, m1, work in rib as set to last 2 sts, m1, rib to end of row. *36 (38: 41: 43: 46) sts, not including 6 sts on stitch holder.*

Change to 3.75mm needles.

Beg with a k row, work in st st from chart A (if working floral motif in intarsia instead of embroidering in duplicate stitch) over the first 31 sts in the row, introducing yarns A and B where required, but AT THE SAME TIME inc 1 st at beg of 5th row and then at beg of 1 (2: 1: 2: 2) foll 24th (16th: 24th: 16th: 18th) rows. *38 (41: 43: 46: 49) sts.*

SHAPE FRONT SLOPE

Keeping floral motif correct (if working in intarsia), dec 1 st at centre front edge of next and every foll 6th (6th: 6th: 5th: 5th) row until Left Front matches Back to beg of armhole shaping, ending with a WS row. *35 (38: 41: 44: 47) sts.*

SHAPE ARMHOLE

NEXT ROW (RS): Cast off 5 (5: 5: 6: 7) sts at beg of row and dec 1 (–: 1: 1: –) sts at end of row. *29 (33: 35: 37: 40) sts.*

Work 1 row.

Dec 1 st at armhole edge of next 3 (3: 3: 3: 5) rows, then on 1 (2: 3: 3: 2) foll alt rows but AT THE SAME TIME dec 1 st at centre front edge as set on every foll 6th (6th: 6th: 5th: 5th) row since previous dec until 16 (17: 18: 19: 20) sts rem.

Cont to work without shaping until Left Front matches Back to beg of shoulder shaping, ending with a WS row.

SHAPE SHOULDER

Cast off 5 (6: 6: 6: 7) sts at beg of next row.

Work 1 row.

Cast off 5 (6: 6: 7: 6) sts at beg of next row.

Work 1 row.

Cast off rem 6 (5: 6: 6: 7) sts.

TO MAKE RIGHT FRONT

Using 3.75mm needles and MC, cast on 40 (42: 45: 47: 50) sts.

ROW I (RS): * K2, p2; rep from * to last 0 (2: 1: 3: 2) sts, k 0 (2: 1: 2: 2), p 0 (0: 0: 1: 0).

ROW 2: K 0 (0: 0: 1: 0), p 0 (2: 1: 2: 2), * k2, p2; rep from * to end of row.

ROW 3 (BUTTONHOLE): K2, cast off next 2 sts, rib as set to end of row.

ROW 4 (BUTTONHOLE): K 0 (0: 0: 1: 0), p 0 (2: 1: 2: 2), * k2, p2; rep from * to last 2 sts, cast on 2 sts over those cast off in previous row (see instructions given on page 63), p2.

Cont to work in rib as set for a further 10 rows.

Change to 3mm needles.

Cont to work in rib as set for a further 4 rows.

Repeat Rows 3 and 4 to make a second buttonhole.

Cont to work in rib as set for a further 9 rows.

NEXT ROW (WS): Rib 2 sts as set, m1, rib as set to last 8 sts, m1, rib as set to end of row. *42 (44: 47: 49: 52) sts.*

NEXT ROW (RS): Rib 6 sts as set, place sts just worked on a stitch holder or safety pin, change to 3.75mm needles and k to end of row. *36 (38: 41: 43: 46) sts, not including 6 sts on stitch holder.*

Cont to work in st st as given for Left Front, following chart B (if working floral motif in intarsia rather than embroidering in duplicate stitch at the end) and reversing all shaping.

ADD SURFACE EMBROIDERY TO LEFT AND RIGHT FRONTS

Using duplicate stitch (see instructions given on page 129) and yarns A and B, embroider the floral motifs over the surface of the Left and Right Fronts following charts A and B on pages 94 and 95.

Using a combination of cross stitch in yarns C and D and French knots in yarns E, F and G, work additional surface embroidery around the mustard and pink floral motifs. Using whipped backstitch in yarns H and I, work additional surface embroidery to add stems to the flowers.

TO MAKE THE SLEEVES (MAKE TWO)

Using 3mm needles and MC, cast on 41 (43: 45: 47: 49) sts.
Work 16 rows in double rib (k2, p2 rib) as given for 3rd
(4th: 3rd: 4th: 3rd) size for Left Front.
Change to 3.75mm needles and beg with a k row work in
st st but AT THE SAME TIME inc 1 st at each end of next
row and 3 foll alt rows. *49 (51: 53: 55: 57) sts.*
Cont to work in st st without shaping for 2 further rows.
Cont to work in st st but AT THE SAME TIME inc 1 st at
each end of next row and every foll 13th (12th: 11th: 10th:
9th) row until there are 65 (69: 73: 77: 81) sts.
Cont to work in st st without shaping until Sleeve measures
44 (44.5: 45: 45.5: 46)cm, ending with a WS row.

SHAPE SLEEVEHEAD
Cast off 5 (5: 5: 6: 7) sts at beg of next 2 rows.
55 (59: 63: 65: 67) sts.
Cont to work in st st but AT THE SAME TIME dec 1 st at
each end of rows as folls:

FOR 1ST SIZE ONLY
next 3 rows, 3 foll alt rows, foll 4th row, foll 5th row, foll
4th row, foll 5th row, foll alt row, foll 3rd row, 3 foll alt
rows, next 2 rows. *21 sts.*

FOR 2ND SIZE ONLY
next 4 rows, 2 foll 3rd rows, 2 foll 4th rows, foll 5th row,
2 foll 4th rows, foll 3rd row, 3 foll alt rows, next row, then
cast off 3 sts at beg of next 2 rows. *21 sts.*

FOR 3RD SIZE ONLY
next 4 rows, foll 3rd row, foll 4th row, 2 foll 6th rows, foll
7th row, foll 4th row, 3 foll alt rows, next 4 rows, then
cast off 4 sts at beg of next 2 rows. *21 sts.*

FOR 4TH SIZE ONLY
next 4 rows, foll 3rd row, foll 4th row, 2 foll 7th rows, foll
5th row, foll 4th row, 5 foll alt rows, next 3 rows, then
cast off 4 sts at beg of next 2 rows. *21 sts.*

FOR 5TH SIZE ONLY
next 5 rows, foll 4th row, 2 foll 8th rows, foll 7th row, foll
5th row, foll 3rd row, 3 foll alt rows, next 2 rows, then
cast off 3 sts at beg of next 2 rows and cast off 4 sts at beg
of next 2 rows. *21 sts.*

ALL SIZES
Cast off rem 21 sts.

TO MAKE UP
Join shoulder seams using mattress stitch or backstitch.

WORK LEFT FRONT BUTTONBAND AND COLLAR
Using 3mm needles and with RS facing, rejoin yarn MC to
6 sts held on stitch holder at Left Front.
Work 4 rows in k2, p2 rib as set.
Cont to work in k2, p2 rib as set but AT THE SAME TIME
inc 1 st at end of next and every foll 8th row until there are
12 sts, incorporating all inc sts into double rib.
Then inc 1 st at end of every foll 4th until there are 18 sts.
Then inc 1 st at end of every alt row until there are 38 sts.
Cont to work in rib as set without shaping until
buttonband and collar when slightly stretched matches
centre back neck.
Cast off in rib.

WORK RIGHT FRONT BUTTONHOLE BAND AND COLLAR
Using 3mm needles and with WS facing, rejoin yarn MC
to 6 sts held on stitch holder at Right Front.
Work 1 row in k2, p2 rib as set.
ROW I (BUTTONHOLE): K2, cast off next 2 sts, k to end
of row.
ROW 2 (BUTTONHOLE): P2, cast on 2 sts over those cast
off in previous row, p2.
Cont to work in double rib as set but AT THE SAME TIME
inc 1 st at beg of next and every foll 8th row until there
are 12 sts, then inc 1 st at beg of every foll 4th until there
are 18 sts, then inc 1 st at beg of every alt row until there
are 38 sts incorporating all inc sts into double rib and AT
THE SAME TIME make a buttonhole every 14th row until 5
buttonholes have been made.
NOTE: Always work cast-off stitches for buttonhole two
sts in from edge of buttonhole band, adjusting accordingly
to accommodate inc sts.
Cont to work in double rib as set without shaping until
buttonhole band and collar when slightly stretched
matches centre back neck.
Cast off in rib.

TO FINISH
Slip stitch buttonbands and collars in place along Left and
Right Front edges, joining cast-off ends together at centre
back neck.
Set in the sleeves, matching the centre points of the
sleeveheads to the shoulder seams.
Join side and sleeve seams using mattress stitch.
Sew buttons securely onto Left Front buttonband to
correspond with buttonholes on Right Front.

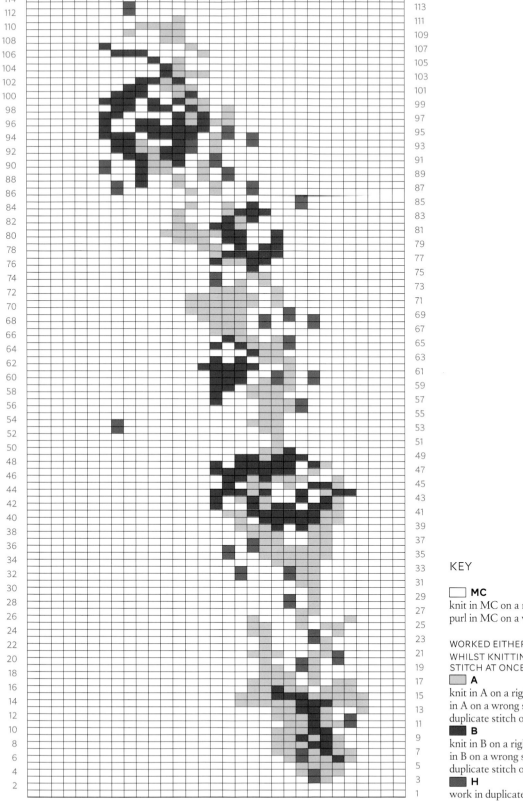

KEY

☐ **MC**
knit in MC on a right side row and
purl in MC on a wrong side row

WORKED EITHER IN INTARISA
WHILST KNITTING OR IN DUPLICATE
STITCH AT ONCE KNITTED

▩ **A**
knit in A on a right side row and purl
in A on a wrong side row or work in
duplicate stitch over MC

■ **B**
knit in B on a right side row and purl
in B on a wrong side row or work in
duplicate stitch over MC

■ **H**
work in duplicate stitch over MC

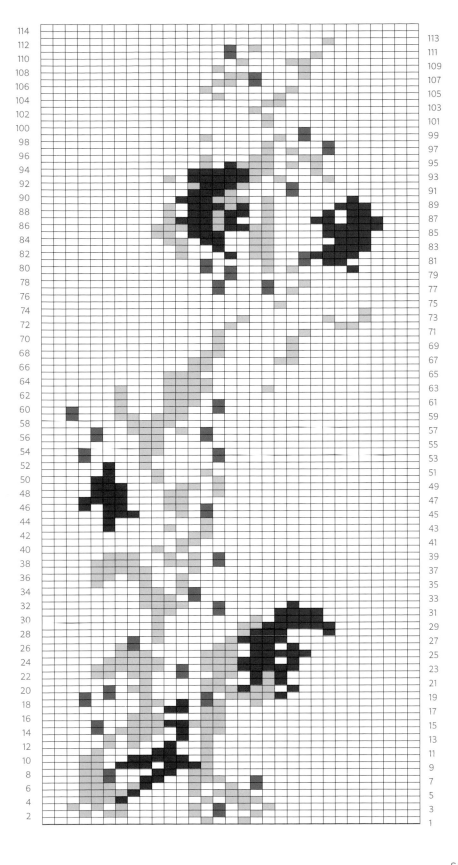

FAIR ISLE BAND SWEATER
WITH SHORT SLEEVES

 love

SIZE

UK	8	10	12	14	16
TO FIT BUST (CM)	81	86	91	97	102
TO FIT BUST (IN)	32	34	36	38	40
ACTUAL BUST (CM)	82.5	87.5	92.5	97.5	102.5
ACTUAL BUST (IN)	33	35	37	39	41
LENGTH (CM)	50.5	51	51.5	54	57.5
LENGTH (IN)	20	20¼	20½	21¼	22¾
SLEEVE SEAM (CM)	10	10	10	10	10
SLEEVE SEAM (IN)	4	4	4	4	4

YARN

Double-knitting weight wool yarn, such as Jamieson's
  Double Knitting, in the following colours:
A 6 (6: 7: 8: 8) x 25g balls in plum (Plum)
B 5 (5: 6: 7: 7) x 25g balls in mustard (Mustard)
Pair each of size 3.5mm and 3.75mm knitting needles
3.5mm circular knitting needle
Stitch holder
Tapestry needle

TENSION

25 sts and 32 rows to 10cm square worked over stocking
stitch on 3.75mm needles. Adjust needle size as necessary
to obtain tension.

ABBREVIATIONS

See standard abbreviations on page 9.

TO MAKE THE BACK

Using 3.5mm needles and A, cast on 99 (105: 111: 117:
123) sts.
ROW I (RS): * K1, p1; rep from * to last st, k1.
ROW 2: * P1, k1; rep from * to last st, p1.
The last two rows form the single rib (k1, p1 rib) pattern.
Cont to work in single rib as set until Back measures 5cm
from cast-on edge, ending with a WS row.
Change to 3.75mm needles.
NEXT ROW (RS): K to end of row.
NEXT ROW: P to end of row.
The last two rows form the stocking stitch (st st) pattern.
Cont to work in st st as set until Back measures 28 (28:
28: 30: 32)cm from cast-on edge, ending with a WS row.
Beg with a k row, work 12 rows in st st following chart A
(see chart notes), introducing yarn B where required.

FOR 1ST AND 2ND SIZES ONLY
Cont to work in st st in B only for a further 2.5cm, ending
with a WS row.

SHAPE ARMHOLES

FOR 1ST SIZE ONLY
Cast off 4 sts at beg of next 2 rows.
Cast off 2 sts at beg of next 4 rows.
Cast off 1 st at beg of next 2 rows. *81 (–: –: –: –) sts.*

FOR 2ND SIZE ONLY
Cast off 4 sts at beg of next 2 rows.
Cast off 2 sts at beg of next 8 rows. *– (81: –: –: –) sts.*

FOR 3RD SIZE ONLY
Cast off 4 sts at beg of next 2 rows.
Cast off 2 sts at beg of next 10 rows. *– (–: 83: –: –) sts.*

FOR 4TH AND 5TH SIZES ONLY
Cast off 6 sts at beg of next 2 rows.
Cast off 2 sts at beg of next 10 (12) rows. *– (–: –: 85: 87) sts.*
* *

ALL SIZES
Cont to work in st st until Back measures 50.5 (51: 51.5:
54: 57.5)cm from cast-on edge, ending with a WS row.

WORKING FAIR ISLE COLOUR CHANGES

STEP 1 On both knit and purl rows, work as usual to the point of the first colour change.

STEP 2 Drop the working yarn and bring the new colour yarn over the top of the dropped yarn. Work as usual to the next colour change.

STEP 3 Drop the working yarn and bring the new yarn under the dropped yarn. Work to the next colour change. Repeat these two steps for all subsequent colour changes.

SHAPE SHOULDERS
Cast off 7 (7: 8: 8: 8) sts at beg of next 6 (6: 4: 4: 6) rows.
Slip remaining 39 sts onto a stitch holder.

TO MAKE THE FRONT
Work as given for Back until **.
Cont to work in st st until Front measures 44 (44: 44: 46: 48)cm from cast-on edge, ending with a WS row.

SHAPE FRONT NECK
NEXT ROW (RS): K28 (28: 29: 30: 31), turn, leave rem unworked sts on a stitch holder.
Cont to work in st st on these 28 (28: 29: 30: 31) sts only to create left front of neck but AT THE SAME TIME dec 1st at neck edge of next 7 alt rows. *21 (21: 22: 23: 24) sts.*
Cont to work in st st without shaping until Front measures 50.5 (51: 51.5: 54: 57.5)cm from cast-on edge, ending with a WS row.

SHAPE SHOULDER
Cast off 7 (7: 8: 8: 8) sts at beg of next and 2 (2: 1: 1: 2) foll alt rows.

FOR 3RD AND 4TH SIZES ONLY
Cast off – (–: 6: 7: –) sts at beg of next 2 rows.

ALL SIZES
Leave centre 25 sts on a stitch holder and rejoin yarn to unworked stitches to work right front of neck.
Knit 1 row.
Work to match left front of neck, reversing all shaping.

TO MAKE THE SLEEVES (MAKE TWO)
Using 3.5mm needles and A, cast on 67 (71: 75: 79: 83) sts.
Work 1.5cm in single rib as given for Back ending with a WS row.
Change to 3.75m needles.
Beg with a k row, work 12 rows in st st following chart B, introducing yarn B where required but AT THE SAME TIME inc 1st at sleeve edges where indicated. *81 (85: 89: 93: 97) sts.*

SHAPE SLEEVEHEAD
Cont to work in st st in B only, cast off 4 (4: 4: 6: 6) sts at beg of next 2 rows.
Cast off 4 (4: 4: 2: 2) sts at beg of next 2 rows.
ROW 1 (RS): * K1, skpo, k to last 3 sts, k2tog, k1.
ROW 2: P to end of row.
Rep last two rows until 29 (31: 33: 35: 37) sts rem.
Cast off 3 sts at beg of next 4 rows.
Cast off rem 17 (19: 21: 23: 25) sts.

TO MAKE UP

Weave in any loose yarn ends on wrong side of work.
Join the shoulder seams using backstitch.
Using 3.5mm circular needle and B, with RS facing and
starting at left shoulder seam, pick up 31 sts down left
front neck, 25 sts from stitch holder at centre front neck,
31 sts up right front neck to right shoulder seam, 39 sts
from stitch holder at centre back neck. *126 sts.*
Working in rounds, cont to work in single rib as given
for Back for 6 rounds.
Cast off loosely in rib.

CHART A NOTES
For right side (knit) rows, read chart
from right to left and for wrong side
(purl) rows, read chart from left to right.

CHART A
BACK AND FRONT

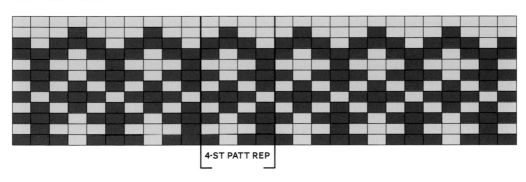

4-ST PATT REP

CHART B
SLEEVES

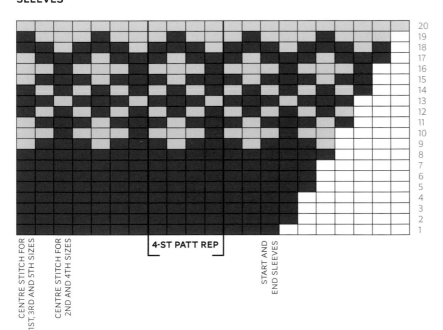

20 19 18 17 16 15 14 13 12 11 10 9 8 7 6 5 4 3 2 1

CHART B NOTES
For both right side (knit)
rows and wrong side (purl)
rows, read chart from right
to left up to centre stitch,
work centre stitch, then
work back from left to right.

CENTRE STITCH FOR
1ST, 3RD AND 5TH SIZES

CENTRE STITCH FOR
2ND AND 4TH SIZES

4-ST PATT REP

START AND
END SLEEVES

TEXTURED CARDIGAN
WITH RIBBED WAIST

SIZE

UK	6	8	10	12	14
TO FIT BUST (CM)	76	81	86	91	97
TO FIT BUST (IN)	30	32	34	36	38
ACTUAL BUST (CM)	80	85	90	95	100
ACTUAL BUST (IN)	31½	33½	35½	37½	39¼
LENGTH (CM)	53.5	55.5	57.5	59.5	61.5
LENGTH (IN)	21	22	22½	23½	24¼
SLEEVE SEAM (CM)	43	44	45	46	47
SLEEVE SEAM (IN)	17	17½	17¾	18	18½

YOU WILL NEED
10 (11: 12: 13: 14) x 50g hanks any double-knitting weight
   wool yarn, such as Frog Tree Alpaca Sport Melange, in
   deep pink (Pumpkin Melange)
Pair each of 3mm and 3.25mm knitting needles
6 (6: 6: 7: 7) small buttons
Tapestry needle

TENSION
24.5 sts x 40 rows to 10cm square over stitch pattern
using 3.25mm needles. Adjust needle size as necessary to
obtain tension.

ABBREVIATIONS
SK2PO slip 1 stitch, knit 2 stitches, pass slipped stitch over
See standard abbreviations on page 7.

PATTERN NOTE
Throughout this cardigan the lace and ridge stitch panel
patterns are worked alternately. As the number of stitches
are decreased and increased, adjust the pattern panels
accordingly to accommodate the lost or gained stitches.

LACE PANEL
(4-ROW REPEAT WORKED OVER 7 STS)
ROW 1: K1, [yfwd, sk2po] twice.
ROW 2: Purl.
ROW 3: [Sk2po, yfwd] twice, k1.
ROW 4: Purl.

RIDGE STITCH PANEL
(4-ROW REPEAT WORKED OVER 6 STS)
ROWS 1, 3 AND 4: K6.
ROW 2: P6.

TO MAKE A TENSION SWATCH
Work sample over lace and ridge stitch patterns, as folls:
Using 3.25mm needles, cast on 26 sts.
ROW 1: K3, k1, [yfwd, sk2po] twice, k6, k1, [yfwd, sk2po]
twice, k3.
ROW 2: P to end of row.
ROW 3: K3, [sk2po, yfwd] twice, k1, k6, [sk2po, yfwd]
twice, k1, k3.
ROW 4: K3, p7, k6, p7, k3.
Rep last four rows until swatch measures 10cm or larger.

TO MAKE THE BACK
Using 3mm needles, cast on 99 (105: 111: 117: 123) sts.
ROW 1: * K1, p1; rep from * to last st, k1.
ROW 2: * K1, p1; rep from * to last st, k1.
These two rows set the moss stitch (moss st) pattern.
Cont to work in moss st for a further 10 rows but AT THE
SAME TIME dec 1 st at each end of 7th (7th: 7th: 8th: 8th)
row. *97 (103: 109: 115: 121)* sts.
Change to 3.25mm needles.
The following rows set the lace and ridge stitch patterns:

FOR 1ST SIZE ONLY
ROW 1 (RS): K6, * k1, [yfwd, sk2po] twice, k6; rep from *
to end of row.
ROW 2: P to end.

ROW 3: K6, * [sk2po, yfwd] twice, k1, k6; rep from * to end of row.
ROW 4: K6, * p7, k6; rep from * to end of row.

FOR 2ND SIZE ONLY
ROW 1 (RS): K9, * k1, [yfwd, sk2po] twice, k6; rep from * to last 3 sts, k3.
ROW 2: P to end.
ROW 3: K9, * [sk2po, yfwd] twice, k1, k6; rep from * to last 3 sts, k3.
ROW 4: P3, k6, * p7, k6, rep from * to last 3 sts, p3.

FOR 3RD SIZE ONLY
ROW 1 (RS): K12, * k1, [yfwd, sk2po] twice, k6; rep from * to last 6 sts, k6.
ROW 2: P to end.
ROW 3: K12, * [sk2po, yfwd] twice, k1, k6; rep from * to last 6 sts, k6.
ROW 4: P6, k6, * p7, k6; rep from last 6 sts, p6.

FOR 4TH SIZE ONLY
ROW 1 (RS): K2, * k1, [yfwd, sk2po] twice, k6; rep from * to last 9 sts, k1, [yfwd, sk2po] twice, k2.
ROW 2: P to end.
ROW 3: K2, * [sk2po, yfwd] twice, k1, k6; rep from * to last 9 sts, [sk2po, yfwd] twice, k1, k2.
ROW 4: K2, * p7, k6; rep from * to last 9 sts, p7, k2.

FOR 5TH SIZE ONLY
ROW 1 (RS): K5, * k1, [yfwd, sk2po] twice, k6; rep from * to last 12 sts, k1, [yfwd, sk2po] twice, k5.
ROW 2: P to end.
ROW 3: K5, * [sk2po, yfwd] twice, k1, k6; rep from * to last 12 sts, [sk2po, yfwd] twice, k1, k5.
ROW 4: K5, * p7, k6; rep from * to last 12 sts, p7, k5.

FOR ALL SIZES
These four rows set the lace and ridge stitch patterns.
Rep last four rows until work measures 16.5 (17: 17.5: 18: 18.5)cm, ending with a WS row, but AT THE SAME TIME dec 1 st at each end of next and every foll 6th row until 81 (87: 93: 99: 105) sts rem.

WORK THE RIBBED WAISTBAND
Change to 3mm needles.
ROW 1: K1, * p1, k1; rep from * to end of row.
ROW 2: P1, * k1, p1; rep from * to end of row.
These two rows set the single rib (k1, p1 rib) pattern.
Cont to work in single rib for a further 18 rows.
Change to 3.25mm needles and beg with Row 1, cont to work four-row repeat patt as before, maintaining

placement of each panel as set prior to ribbed waistband, until work measures 13 (13.5: 14: 14.5: 15)cm from top of ribbed waistband, ending with a WS row, but AT THE SAME TIME inc 1 st at each end of every 5th row until there are 99 (105: 111: 117: 123) sts.

SHAPE ARMHOLES
Cast off 3 (4: 4: 4: 5) sts at beg of next two rows. *93 (97: 103: 109: 113) sts.*

FOR 1ST, 2ND AND 3RD SIZES ONLY
Dec 1 st at each end of next 4 rows. *85 (89: 95: –: –) sts.*
Dec 1 st at each end of next 1 (1: 2: –: –) foll 4th (alt: alt: –: –) rows. *83 (87: 91: –: –) sts.*
Dec 1 st at each end of foll 8th (4th: –: –: –) rows. *81 (85: 91: –: –) sts.*

FOR 3RD SIZE ONLY
Dec 1 st at each end of 2 foll 4th rows. *– (–: 87: –: –) sts.*

FOR 4TH AND 5TH SIZES ONLY
Cast off 2 sts at beg of next – (–: –: 6: 6) rows. *– (–: –: 97: 101) sts.*
Dec 1 st at each end of next row. *– (–: –: 95: 99) sts.*
Dec 1 st at each end of foll alt row. *– (–: –: 93: 97) sts.*
Dec 1 st at each end of foll – (–: –: 6th: 4th) row. *– (–: –: 91: 95) sts.*

FOR 5TH SIZE ONLY
Dec 1 st at each end of foll 5th row. *– (–: –: –: 93) sts.*

FOR ALL SIZES
Cont to work in patt without shaping until armhole measures 19 (20: 21: 22: 23)cm ending with a WS row. *81 (85: 87: 91: 93) sts.*

SHAPE BACK NECK AND SHOULDERS
NEXT ROW (RS): Patt until there are 26 (28: 29: 31: 32) sts on RH needle, turn and leave rem unworked sts on a stitch holder.
Work each side of the neck separately.
Cast off 3 sts at beg of next row. *23 (25: 26: 28: 29) sts.*
Dec 1 st at beg of foll alt row. *22 (24: 25: 27: 28) sts.*
Cast off 7 (7: 8: 8: 9) sts at beg and dec 1 st at end of next row. *14 (16: 16: 18: 18) sts.*
Dec 1 st at beg of next row. *13 (15: 15: 17: 17) sts.*
Cast off 6 (7: 7: 8: 8) sts at beg and dec 1 st at end of next row. *6 (7: 7: 8: 8) sts.*
Work 1 row.
Cast off rem 6 (7: 7: 8: 8) sts.
With RS facing, rejoin yarn to stitches from stitch holder.

NEXT ROW: Cast off centre 29 sts, patt to end. *26 (28: 29: 31: 32)sts.*

Complete to match first side of neck, reversing all shaping.

TO MAKE LEFT FRONT

Using 3mm needles, cast on 54 (57: 60: 63: 66) sts.

ROW 1: P – (1: –: 1: –), * k1, p1; rep from * to end of row.

ROW 2: * P1, k1; rep from * to last – (1: –: 1: –)sts, p – (1: –: 1: –).

These two rows set the moss stitch pattern.

Cont to work in moss st as set for a further 10 rows but AT THE SAME TIME dec 1 st at beg of the 7th (7th: 7th: 8th: 8th) row. *53 (56: 59: 62: 65) sts.*

Change to 3.25mm needles.

The following four rows set the lace and ridge stitch patt and 8-st moss stitch buttonband worked at centre front:

FOR 1ST SIZE ONLY

ROW 1 (RS): K6, * k1, [yfwd, sk2po] twice, k6; rep from * to last 8 sts, [k1, p1] four times.

ROW 2: [P1, k1] four times, p to end of row.

ROW 3: K6, * [sk2po, yfwd] twice, k1, k6; rep from * to last 8 sts, [k1, p1] four times.

ROW 4: [P1, k1] four times, k6, * p7, k6; rep from * to end of row.

FOR 2ND SIZE ONLY

ROW 1 (RS): K9, * k1, [yfwd, sk2po] twice, k6; rep from * to last 8 sts, [k1, p1] four times.

ROW 2: [P1, k1] four times, p to end of row.

ROW 3: K9, * [sk2po, yfwd] twice, k1, k6; rep from * to last 8 sts, [k1, p1] four times.

ROW 4: [P1, k1] four times, k6, * p7, k6; rep from * to last 3 sts, p3.

FOR 3RD SIZE ONLY

ROW 1 (RS): K12, * k1, [yfwd, sk2po] twice, k6, rep from * to last 8 sts, [k1, p1] four times.

ROW 2: [P1, k1] four times, p to end of row.

ROW 3: [Sk2po, yfwd] twice, k6, * [sk2po, yfwd] twice, k1, k6; rep from * to last 8 sts, [k1, p1] four times.

ROW 4: [P1, k1] four times, k6, * p7, k6; rep from * to last 6 sts, p6.

FOR 4TH SIZE ONLY

ROW 1 (RS): K2, * k1, [yfwd, sk2po] twice, k6; rep from * to last 8 sts, [k1, p1] four times.

ROW 2: [P1, k1] four times, p to end of row.

ROW 3: K2, * [sk2po, yfwd] twice, k1, k6; rep from * to last 8 sts, [k1, p1] four times.

ROW 4: [p1, k1] four times, * k6, p7; rep from * to last 2 sts, k2.

FOR 5TH SIZE ONLY

ROW 1 (RS): K5, * k1, [yfwd, sk2po] twice, k6; rep from * to last 8 sts, [k1, p1] four times.

ROW 2: [P1, k1] four times, p to end of row.

ROW 3: K5, * [sk2po, yfwd] twice, k1, k6; rep from * to last 8 sts, [k1, p1] four times.

ROW 4: [P1, k1] four times, * k6, p7; rep from * to last 5 sts, k5.

FOR ALL SIZES

These four rows set the lace and ridge stitch patt and 8-st moss stitch buttonband.

Rep the last four rows until work measures 16.5 (17: 17.5: 18: 18.5)cm, ending with a WS row, but AT THE SAME TIME dec 1 st at beg of next and every foll 6th row until 45 (48: 51: 54: 57) sts rem.

WORK THE RIBBED WAISTBAND

Change to 3mm needles.

ROW 1: K 1 (–: 1: –: 1), * p1, k1; rep from * to end of row.

ROW 2: * P1, k1; rep from * to last 1 (–: 1: –: 1) sts, p 1 (–: 1: –: 1).

These two rows set the single rib (k1, p1 rib) pattern.

Cont to work in single rib as set for a further 18 rows.

NOTE: Work 8-st buttonband in single rib instead of moss st over 20 rows of ribbed waistband only.

Change to 3.25mm needles.

Beg with Row 1, cont to work four-row repeat patt as before, maintaining placement of each panel and moss stitch buttonband as set prior to working ribbed waistband, until work measures 13 (13.5: 14: 14.5: 15)cm from top of ribbed waistband, ending with a WS row, but AT THE SAME TIME inc 1 st at beg of 5th and at same edge of every foll 5th row until there are 54 (57: 60: 63: 66) sts.

SHAPE ARMHOLE

Cast off 3 (4: 4: 4: 5) sts at beg of next row. *51 (53: 56: 59: 61) sts.*

FOR 1ST, 2ND AND 3RD SIZES ONLY

Dec 1 st at armhole edge of foll alt row. *50 (52: 55: –: –) sts.*

Dec 1 st at armhole edge of next 3 rows. *47 (49: 52: –: –) sts.*

Dec 1 st at armhole edge of 1 (1: 2: –: –) foll 4th (alt: alt: –: –) rows. *46 (48: 50: –: –) sts.*

Dec 1 st at armhole edge of 1 (1: –: –: –) foll 8th (4th: –: –: –) row. *45 (47: 50: –: –) sts.*

FOR 3RD SIZE ONLY
Dec 1 st at armhole edge of 2 foll 4th rows. – (–: 48: –: –) sts.

FOR 4TH AND 5TH SIZES ONLY
Cast off 2 sts at beg of next and 2 foll alt rows. – (–: –: 53: 55) sts.
Dec 1 st at armhole edge of next row. – (–: –: 52: 54) sts.
Dec 1 st at armhole edge of foll 3rd row. – (–: –: 51: 53) sts.
Dec 1 st at armhole edge of foll – (–: –: 6th: 4th) row. – (–: –: 50: 52) sts.

FOR 5TH SIZE ONLY
Dec 1 st at armhole edge of foll 5th row. – (–: –: –: 51) sts.

FOR ALL SIZES
Cont to work in patt without shaping until armhole measures 36 rows fewer than the Back to the point where the shaping of the back neck and shoulders begins, ending with a WS row. 45 (47: 48: 50: 51) sts.

SHAPE FRONT NECK
NEXT ROW (RS): Patt to last 8 sts, turn and leave 8 moss sts on a stitch holder or safety pin.
Cast off 5 sts at beg of next row. 32 (34: 35: 37: 38) sts.
Cast off 2 sts at beg of foll alt row. 30 (32: 33: 35: 36) sts.
Dec 1 st at neck edge of next 4 rows. 26 (28: 29: 31: 32) sts.
Dec 1 st at neck edge of foll 4 alt rows. 22 (24: 25: 27: 28) sts.
Dec 1 st at neck edge of 3 foll 6th rows. 19 (21: 22: 24: 25) sts.
Work 2 rows.

SHAPE SHOULDER
NEXT ROW (RS): Cast off 7 (7: 8: 8: 9) sts, patt to end of row. 12 (14: 14: 16: 16) sts.
Work 1 row in pattern.
NEXT ROW (RS): Cast off 6 (7: 7: 8: 8) sts, patt to end of row. 6 (7: 7: 8: 8) sts.
Work 1 row in patt.
Cast off rem 6 (7: 7: 8: 8) sts.
Mark positions for 6 (6: 6: 7: 7) buttons, placing lowest at centre of ribbed waistband, highest at centre of neckband (this is added later so you need to estimate its position) and the rest evenly spaced between these two.

TO MAKE RIGHT FRONT
Using 3mm needles, cast on 54 (57: 60: 63: 66) sts.
ROW I: * P1, k1; rep from * to last – (1: –: 1: –) sts, p – (1: –: 1: –).
ROW 2: P – (1: –: 1: –), * k1, p1; rep from * to end of row.
These two rows set the moss stitch pattern.
Cont to work in moss st for a further 10 rows but AT THE

SAME TIME dec 1 st at beg of 7th (7th: 7th: 8th: 8th) row. 53 (56: 59: 62: 65) sts.
Change to 3.25mm needles.
Cont to work in patt reversing as set for Left Front with integral moss stitch buttonband at centre front edge, reversing all shaping but AT THE SAME TIME work buttonholes within moss stitch buttonhole band to correspond with marked button positions as folls:

WORK BUTTONHOLE IN RIBBED WAISTBAND
NEXT ROW (RS): Rib 2 sts, rib2tog, yon, rib 4 sts, patt to end of row.

WORK BUTTONHOLE IN MOSS ST BUTTONBAND
NEXT ROW (RS): Moss st 2, k2tog, yrn, moss st 4, patt to end of row.

TO MAKE SLEEVES (MAKE TWO)
Using 3mm needles, cast on 37 (39: 39: 41: 43) sts.
ROW I: * K1, p1; rep from * to last st, k1.
ROW 2: * K1, p1; rep from * to last st, k1.
These two rows set the moss stitch pattern.
Rep last two rows a further five times but AT THE SAME TIME inc 1 st at each end of every 6th (4th: 4th: 4th: 4th) row. 41 (45: 45: 47: 49) sts.
Change to 3.25mm needles.
The following rows set the lace and ridge stitch patterns:

FOR 1ST SIZE ONLY
ROW I (RS): K4, k1, [yfwd, sk2po] twice, * k6, k1, [yfwd, sk2po] twice; rep from * to last 4 sts, k4.
ROW 2: P to end of row.
ROW 3: K4, [sk2po, yfwd] twice, k1, * k6, [sk2po, yfwd] twice, k1; rep from * to last 4 sts, k4.
ROW 4: K4, p7, * k6, p7; rep from * to last 4 sts, k4.

FOR 2ND AND 3RD SIZES ONLY
ROW I (RS): K6, * k1, [yfwd, sk2po] twice, k6; rep from * to end of row.
ROW 2: P to end of row.
ROW 3: K6, * [sk2po, yfwd] twice, k1, k6; rep from * to end of row.
ROW 4: K6, * p7, k6; rep from * to end of row.

FOR 4TH SIZE ONLY
ROW I (RS): K1, k6, * k1, [yfwd, sk2po] twice, k6; rep from * to last st, k1.
ROW 2: P to end of row.
ROW 3: K1, k6, * [sk2po, yfwd] twice, k1, k6; rep from * to last st, k1.
ROW 4: P1, k6, * p7, k6; rep from * to last st, p1.

FOR 5TH SIZE ONLY
ROW 1 (RS): K2, k6, * k1, [yfwd, sk2po] twice, k6; rep from * to last 2 sts, k2.
ROW 2: P to end of row.
ROW 3: K2, k6, * [sk2po, yfwd] twice, k1, k6; rep from * to last 2 sts, k2.
ROW 4: P2, k6, * p7, k6; rep from * to last 2 sts, p2.

FOR ALL SIZES
These four rows set the lace and ridge stitch patterns. Rep these four rows but AT THE SAME TIME inc 1 st at each end of next row and every foll 6th (4th: 4th: 4th: 4th) row until there are 45 (49: 49: 53: 55) sts.

FOR 2ND AND 3RD SIZES ONLY
Work 4 rows without shaping.

FOR ALL SIZES
Cont to work in patt but AT THE SAME TIME inc 1 st at each end of every 6th row until there are 63 (67: 69: 73: 75) sts.
Work a further 14 (14: 7: 7: 7) rows without shaping.
Cont to work in patt but AT THE SAME TIME inc 1 st at each end of every foll 8th (8th: 7th: 7th: 7th) row until there are 81 (87: 91: 97: 101) sts.
Cont to work in patt without shaping until work measures 43 (44: 45: 46: 47)cm.

SHAPE SLEEVEHEAD
Cast off 3 (4: 4: 4: 5) sts at beg of next 2 rows. *75 sts.*

FOR 1ST SIZE ONLY
Keeping patt correct, dec 1 st at each end of next 3 alt rows. Dec 1 st at each end of foll 3rd row, foll 4th row, foll 5th row, foll 4th row, 2 foll 3rd rows, next 9 alt rows, then every row for next 9 rows.

FOR 2ND SIZE ONLY
Keeping patt correct, dec 1 st at each end of next 3 alt rows. Dec 1 st at each end of foll 3rd row, 2 foll 4th rows, 5 foll 3rd rows, 9 foll alt rows, then every row for next 9 rows.

FOR 3RD SIZE ONLY
Keeping patt correct, dec 1 st at each end of next 13 foll 3rd rows, 7 foll alt rows, then every row for next 11 rows.

FOR 4TH SIZE ONLY
Keeping patt correct, dec 1 st at each end of next 2 rows, then foll alt row, 2 foll 3rd rows, foll alt row, 2 foll 3rd rows, 2 foll alt rows, foll 4th row, foll 5th row, 2 foll 3rd rows, 4 foll alt rows, foll 3rd row, 2 foll alt rows, next row, foll alt row, next row, foll alt row, then every row for next 8 rows.

FOR 5TH SIZE ONLY
Keeping patt correct, dec 1 st at each end of next row, then foll 3rd row, 3 foll alt rows, 4 foll 3rd rows, 3 foll 4th rows, 3 foll 3rd rows, 7 foll alt rows, next 3 rows, foll alt row, then every row for next 8 rows.

FOR ALL SIZES
Cast off rcm 21 (21: 21: 23: 23) sts.

TO MAKE UP
Join shoulder seams using either mattress st or backstitch.

WORK NECKBAND
With RS facing and using 3mm needles, pick up and work 8 moss sts from stitch holder at top of buttonhole band on Right Front, then pick up and knit 45 (45: 47: 47: 49) sts along Right Front neck, 41 (41: 44: 44: 46) sts along Back neck, 45 (45: 47: 47: 49) sts from Left Front neck, then pick up and work 8 moss sts from stitch holder at top of buttonband on Left Front. 147 *(147: 154: 154: 160)* sts. Work in moss st for 3 rows.
NEXT ROW (RS): K2, k2tog, yfwd, work in moss st to end. Work in moss st for a further 5 rows.
NEXT ROW (RS): Cast off in moss stitch.

TO FINISH
Set in sleeves using set-in method.
Join side and sleeve seams using mattress stitch.
Sew buttons securely onto Left Front buttonband to correspond with buttonholes on Right Front buttonband.

FAIR ISLE RIB TANKTOP

SIZE

UK	6	8	10	12	14
TO FIT BUST (CM)	76	81	86	91	97
TO FIT BUST (IN)	30	32	34	36	38
ACTUAL BUST (CM)	80	85	90	95	100
ACTUAL BUST (IN)	31½	33½	35½	37½	39½
LENGTH (CM)	43.5	45	51.5	52.5	53.5
LENGTH (IN)	17	17¾	20¼	20¾	21

YARN

MC 4 (5: 6: 7: 8) x 25g balls 4-ply wool yarn, such as
  Jamieson's Spindrift, in ecru (Rye)
4-ply wool yarn, such as Jamieson's Spindrift and
  Patricia Roberts Fine Cotton in the following colours:
A 1 x 25g ball in dark red (Spindrift, Cherry)
B 1 x 25g ball in dark green (Spindrift, Pistachio)
C 1 x 25g ball in yellow (Spindrift, Daffodil)
D 1 x 25g ball in bright pink (Spindrift, Sherbert)
E 1 x 25g ball in turquoise (Spindrift, Splash)
F 1 x 50g ball in bright green (Fine Cotton, Sap)
G 1 x 25g ball in dark blue (Spindrift, Petrol)
Pair each of size 2.75mm and 3.25mm knitting needles

TENSION

30 sts and 32 rows to 10cm square worked over stocking
stitch on 3.25mm needles. Adjust needle size as necessary
to obtain tension.

ABBREVIATIONS

See standard abbreviations on page 9.

PATTERN NOTE

Carry the yarn not being worked along the row on the
wrong side of the work. Do not carry this yarn too tightly
as it will distort the tension of the knitted piece.

TO MAKE THE BACK

Using 2.75mm needles and MC, cast on 113 (121: 129:
137: 145) sts.
ROW 1 (RS): * K1, p1; rep from * to last st, k1.
ROW 2: P1, * k1, p1; rep from * to end of row.
The last two rows form the single rib (k1, p1 rib) pattern.
Cont to work in single rib as set for a further 31 rows,
ending with a RS row.
ROW 1 (INC): Rib 8 (9: 10: 14: 16), inc 1 st, * rib 15 (16: 17:
26: 27), inc 1 st; rep from * to last 8 (9: 10: 14: 16) sts, rib
to end. *120 (128: 136: 142: 150) sts.*
Change to 3.25mm needles.
ROW 1 (RS): * K2, p2; rep from * to last – (–: –: 2: 2) sts,
k – (–: –: 2: 2).
ROW 2: P – (–: –: 2: 2), * k2, p2; rep from * to end of row.
The last two rows form the double rib (k2, p2 rib) pattern.
Cont to work in double rib as set until Back measures 25 (25:
30: 30: 30)cm from cast-on edge, ending with a WS row.

SHAPE ARMHOLES

Keeping rib correct, cast off 4 sts at beg of next 2 rows.
Dec 1 st at each end of next 7 (8: 11: 11: 13) rows. *98 (104:
106: 112: 116) sts.*
Cont to work in double rib as set without shaping until
Back measures 18.5 (20: 21.5: 22.5: 23.5)cm from
armhole shaping, ending with a WS row.

SHAPE SHOULDERS

Cast off 15 (16: 16: 17: 18) sts at beg of next 2 rows.
Cast off 15 (16: 17: 18: 18) sts at beg of next 2 rows.
38 (40: 40: 42: 44) sts.
Change to 2.75mm needles.

Work 9 rows in single rib.
Change to yarn A and work 1 row in single rib.
Cast off in single rib.

TO MAKE THE FRONT

Using 2.75mm needles and MC, cast on 113 (121: 129: 137: 145) sts.
ROW I (RS): * K1, p1; rep from * to last st, k1.
ROW 2: P1, * k1, p1; rep from * to end of row.
These two rows form the single rib (k1, p1 rib) pattern.
Cont to work in single rib for a further 31 rows, ending with a RS row.
Keeping rib correct, inc 20 sts evenly across the next row. *133 (141: 149: 157: 165) sts.*
Change to 3.25mm needles.
ROW I (RS): K to end of row.
ROW 2: P to end of row.
These two rows form the stocking stitch (st st) pattern.
Cont to work in st st following 37-row repeat Fair Isle pattern from chart, starting with Row 1 (1: 17: 17: 17) which is a RS row, work 45 (45: 63: 63: 63) rows.

DIVIDE FOR NECK SHAPING
NEXT ROW (WS): Patt 66 (70: 74: 78: 82) sts, place worked sts on a stitch holder, p2tog, patt to end of row. *66 (70: 74: 78: 82) sts.*

WORK LEFT NECK
Keeping patt correct, dec 1 st at neck edge on foll 7 (7: 8: 8: 8) 3rd rows.
Work 1 (1: –: –: –) rows straight, ending at side edge.

SHAPE LEFT ARMHOLE
Dec 1 st at neck edge on 13 (14: 14: 15: 16) foll 4th rows but AT THE SAME TIME cast off 4 sts at beg of next row and then dec 1 st at armhole edge on next 9 (10: 12: 13: 14) rows. *33 (35: 36: 38: 40) sts.*
Keeping patt correct, cont to work without shaping until armhole measures 18.5 (20: 21.5: 22.5: 23.5)cm, ending with a WS row.

SHAPE LEFT SHOULDER
Cast off 16 (17: 18: 19: 20) sts at beg of next row.
Work 1 further row.
Cast off rem 17 (18: 18: 19: 20) sts.

WORK RIGHT NECK
With RS facing, rejoin yarn to sts on stitch holder.
Work in patt to end of row.
Complete to match left neck, reversing all shaping.

TO MAKE FRONT NECKBAND

Using 2.75mm needles and MC, with RS facing and starting at left front shoulder, pick up and knit 54 (58: 62: 66: 68) sts down left front neck edge and 54 (58: 62: 66: 68) sts up right front neck edge. *108 (116: 124: 132: 136) sts.*
ROW I (WS): * K1, p1; rep from * to end of row.
ROW 2 (RS): * K1, p1; rep from * until 52 (56: 60: 64: 66) sts have been worked, sl1, k1, psso, k2tog, * k1, p1; rep from * to end of row.
Keeping rib correct, cont in single rib but AT THE SAME TIME dec 2 sts at centre neck as set on foll 3 alt rows. *100 (108: 116: 124: 128) sts.*
Change to A, work 1 row in single rib.
Cast off in rib.

TO MAKE UP
Weave in any yarn ends carefully on the WS of the work.
NOTE: Lightly spray the finished knitting with water, shape the garment to the correct dimensions and leave to dry flat. Do NOT press the ribbed back.
Join the shoulder seams and neckbands using mattress stitch or back stitch.

WORK ARMBANDS
Using 2.75mm needles and MC, with RS facing and starting at one side edge, pick up and knit 101 (107: 114: 120: 126) sts evenly along armhole edge.
Work 6 rows in single rib.
Change to A and work 1 row in single rib.
Cast off in rib.
Join side seams and armband edges using mattress stitch.

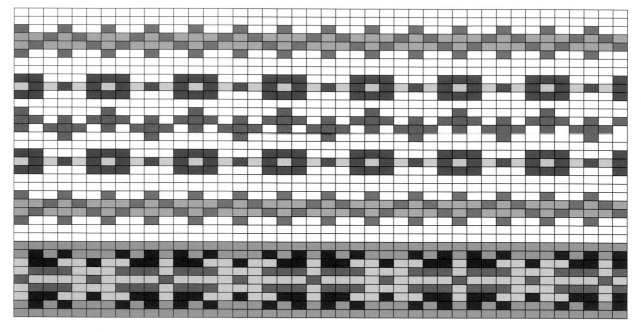

CHART NOTES

For both right side (knit)
rows and wrong side (purl)
rows, read chart from right
to left up to centre stitch,
work centre stitch, then
work back from left to right
to marked line for size being
worked to complete the row.

"FAIR ISLE KNITTING IS A
TRADITIONAL WAY to use up scraps
of yarn. I really love the thrifty aspect of
this technique. You don't actually need
a lot of each colour, so you can use up
oddments you have left over from other
projects to create some lovely, quirky
colour combinations."

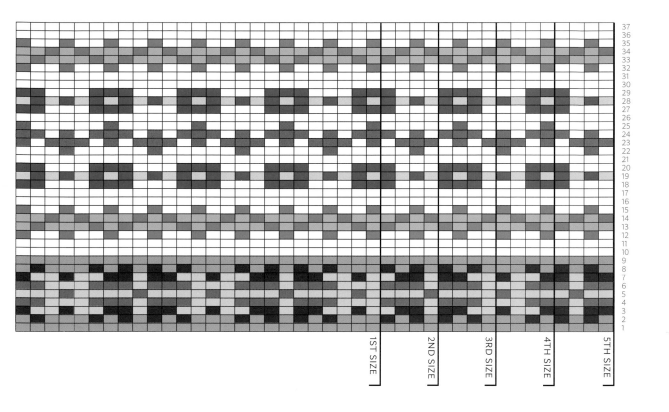

KEY

☐ **MC** (ECRU)
knit in MC on a right side row and purl in MC on a wrong side row.

■ **A** (DARK RED)
knit in A on a right side row and purl in A on a wrong side row.

■ **B** (DARK GREEN)
knit in B on a right side row and purl in B on a wrong side row.

■ **C** (YELLOW)
knit in C on a right side row and purl in C on a wrong side row.

■ **D** (BRIGHT PINK)
knit in D on a right side row and purl in D on a wrong side row.

■ **E** (TURQUOISE)
knit in E on a right side row and purl in E on a wrong side row.

■ **F** (BRIGHT GREEN)
knit in F on a right side row and purl in F on a wrong side row.

■ **G** (DARK BLUE)
knit in G on a right side row and purl in G on a wrong side row.

CABLED TAM AND SNOOD

SIZE
One size, to fit average size woman's head and neck

YOU WILL NEED
FOR TAM
2 x 50g balls double-knitting weight wool yarn, such as
  Artesano DK Superfine Alpaca in dark red (Chile)
FOR SNOOD
3 x 50g balls double-knitting weight wool yarn, such as
  Artesano DK Superfine Alpaca in dark red (Chile)
One each of 3.25mm and 3.75mm circular needle,
  40cm long
Set of four 3.25mm double-pointed knitting needles
Cable needle

TENSION
24 sts and 32 rows to 10cm square worked over stocking
stitch on 3.75mm needles. Adjust needle size as necessary
to obtain tension.

> " IF YOU ARE PLANNING
> ON MAKING BOTH these
> accessories, then I recommend starting
> with the snood. It is a simple straight
> tube of knitting so allows you to perfect
> the cable pattern before moving on to
> the slightly more complex tam, which
> is shaped by regularly decreasing
> stitches over the rounds. "

ABBREVIATIONS
C4B slip next 2 stitches onto cable needle and hold at
back of work, knit next 2 stitches from left-hand needle,
knit 2 stitches from cable needle
C4F slip next 2 stitches onto cable needle and hold at
front of work, knit next 2 stitches from left-hand needle,
knit 2 stitches from cable needle
MAKE BOBBLE (k1, p1, k1, p1, k1) into next stitch, turn,
p5, turn, pass second, third, fourth and fifth stitches over
first stitch, turn, knit into back of first stitch
S2TOGKPO slip 2 stitches together, knit 1 stitch, pass 2
slipped stitches over
T4B slip next 2 stitches onto cable needle and hold at back
of work, knit next 2 stitches from left-hand needle, purl 2
stitches from cable needle
T4F slip next 2 stitches onto cable needle and hold at front
of work, purl next 2 stitches from left-hand needle, knit 2
stitches from cable needle
See also standard abbreviations on page 9.

40-ROW CABLE PATTERN
ROUND I: * P2, k9, p4, k2, p2, k4, p2, k2, p2; rep from *
to end.
ROUND 2: * P2, k9, p4, k2, p2, k4, p2, k2, p2; rep from
* to end.
ROUND 3: * P2, C4B, k1, C4F, p4, k2, p2, C4B, p2, k2,
p2; rep from * to end.
ROUND 4: * P2, k9, p4, k2, p2, k4, p2, k2, p2; rep from
* to end.
ROUND 5: * P2, k4, make bobble, k4, p4, k2, p2, k4, p2,
k2, p2; rep from * to end.
ROUND 6: * P2, k9, p4, k2, p2, k4, p2, k2, p2; rep from
* to end.
ROUND 7: * P2, k3, make bobble, k1, make bobble, k3,
p4, T4F, C4B, T4B, p2; rep from * to end.
ROUND 8: * P2, k9, p6, k8, p4; rep from * to end.
ROUND 9: * p2, k9, p6, T4B, T4F, p4; rep from * to end.
ROUND I0: * P2, k9, p6, k2, p4, k2, p4; rep from * to end.

ROUND 11: * P2, C4B, k1, C4F, p4, T4B, p4, T4F, p2; rep from * to end.

ROUND 12: * P2, k9, p4, k2, p8, k2, p2; rep from * to end.

ROUND 13: * p2, k4, make bobble, k4, p4, k2, p8, k2, p2; rep from * to end.

ROUND 14: * P2, k9, p4, k2, p8, k2, p2; rep from * to end.

ROUND 15: * P2, k3, make bobble, k1, make bobble, k3, p4, T4F, p4, T4B, p2; rep from * to end.

ROUND 16: * P2, k9, p6, k2, p4, k2, p4; rep from * to end.

ROUND 17: * P2, k9, p6, T4F, T4B, p4; rep from * to end.

ROUND 18: * P2, k9, p6, k8, p4; rep from * to end.

ROUND 19: * P2, C4B, k1, C4F, p4, T4B, C4B, T4F, p2; rep from * to end.

ROUND 20: * P2, k9, p4, k2, p2, k4, p2, k2, p2; rep from * to end.

ROUND 21: * P2, k4, make bobble, k4, p4, k2, p2, k4, p2, k2, p2; rep from * to end.

ROUND 22: * P2, k9, p4, k2, p2, k4, p2, k2, p2; rep from * to end.

ROUND 23: * P2, k3, make bobble, k1, make bobble, k3, p4, k2, p2, C4B, p2, k2, p2; rep from * to end.

ROUND 24: * p2, k9, p4, k2, p2, k4, p2, k2, p2; rep from * to end.

ROUND 25: * P2, k9, p4, k2, p2, k4, p2, k2, p2; rep from * to end.

ROUND 26: * P2, k9, p4, k2, p2, k4, p2, k2, p2; rep from * to end.

ROUND 27: * P2, C4B, k1, C4F, p4, T4F, C4B, T4B, p2; rep from * to end.

ROUND 28: * P2, k9, p6, k8, p4; rep from * to end.

ROUND 29: * P2, k4, make bobble, k4, p6, T4B, T4F, p4; rep from * to end.

ROUND 30: * P2, k9, p6, k2, p4, k2, p4; rep from * to end.

ROUND 31: * P2, k3, make bobble, k1, make bobble, k3, p4, T4B, p4, T4F, p2; rep from * to end.

ROUND 32: * P2, k9, p4, k2, p8, k2, p2; rep from * to end.

ROUND 33: * P2, k9, p4, k2, p8, k2, p2; rep from * to end.

ROUND 34: * P2, k9, p4, k2, p8, k2, p2; rep from * to end.

ROUND 35: * P2, C4B, k1, C4F, p4, T4F, p4, T4B, p2; rep from * to end.

ROUND 36: * P2, k9, p6, k2, p4, k2, p4; rep from * to end.

ROUND 37: * P2, k4, make bobble, k4, p6, T4F, T4B, p4; rep from * to end.

ROUND 38: * P2, k9, p6, k8, p4; rep from * to end.

ROUND 39: * P2, k3, make bobble, k1, make bobble, k3, p4, T4B, C4B, T4F, p2; rep from * to end.

ROUND 40: * P2, k9, p4, k2, p2, k4, p2, k2, p2; rep from * to end.

TO MAKE THE SNOOD

Using 3.25mm circular needle, cast on 174 sts.
Cont to work in the round following cable patt as folls:
Work rows 1–10 using 3.25mm circular needle.
Work rows 11–40 using 3.75mm circular needle.
Work rows 1–30 using 3.75mm circular needle.
Work rows 31–40 using 3.25mm circular needle.
Cast off loosely in patt.

TO MAKE THE TAM

Using 3.25mm circular needle, cast on 132 sts.
Cont to work in the round as folls:

ROUND 1: * K2, p2; rep from * to end of round.
This round forms the double rib (k2, p2 rib) pattern.
Cont in double rib as set for a further 7 rounds.

NEXT ROUND: K to end of round, inc 71 sts evenly over round by working into front and back of inc sts. *203 sts.*
Change to 3.75mm circular needle.
Cont to work in cable patt until Tam measures 9cm from top of rib.

NEXT ROUND: Break yarn and rejoin 23 sts back on previous round – this now the beg of next round. (The central stitch of 9-st bobble cable is now the first stitch. Divide round into 7 equal sections of 29 sts and place a stitch marker at beg of each section.

SHAPING THE CROWN

Cont to work in cable patt but AT THE SAME TIME dec as folls adjusting patt for dec sts and changing to double-ended needles when too few sts to work on circular needle:

ROUND 1: * Patt 14, s2togkpo, patt 12; rep from * to end.

ROUND 2 AND ALL EVEN-NUMBERED ROUNDS: * Patt to end.

ROUND 3: * Patt 13, s2togkpo, patt 11; rep from * to end.

ROUND 5: * Patt 12, s2togkpo, patt 10; rep from * to end.

ROUND 7: * Patt 11, s2togkpo, patt 9; rep from * to end.

ROUND 9: * Patt 10, s2togkpo, patt 8; rep from * to end.

ROUND 11 AND ALL ODD-NUMBERED ROUNDS: Cont to work dec rounds as set working one less stitch either side of double decrease than on previous dec round.
Dec until 21 sts rem.

NEXT ROUND: * S2togkpo; rep from * to end of round.
Break off yarn leaving a long tail. Thread tail through rem sts and fasten off.
Weave in any yarn ends on wrong side of finished tam.

POLKA-DOT SOCKS

 love

SIZE
One size: To fit woman's UK shoe size 5–7

YOU WILL NEED
MC 1 x 100g hank 4ply wool yarn, such as
MadelineTosh Tosh Sock, in turquoise (Clover)
A 1 x 50g hank double-knitting weight wool yarn,
such as Koigu Premium Merino yarn in coral (Coral)
Set each of size 2.25mm and 2.75mm double-pointed
knitting needles
Darning needle

TENSION
26 sts to 10cm measured over stocking stitch on 2.75mm
needles. Adjust needle size as necessary to obtain tension.

ABBREVIATIONS
See standard abbreviations on page 9.

> **"YOU CAN KNIT THESE
> POLKA-DOT SOCKS** in any
> colourway that you like. As the
> embroidery is added once the
> knitting is finished, you can play
> around with applying different
> finishing touches with coloured yarns
> in a variety of stitches and patterns.**"**

TO MAKE THE SOCKS (MAKE TWO)
Using 2.25mm double-pointed needles and A, cast on
78 sts. Arrange sts so there are 22 sts on the first needle,
17 sts on the second needle, 17 sts on the third needle and
22 sts on the fourth needle.
Join in a round and mark beg of round with a stitch marker.
Break off A and join in MC.
NEXT ROUND: K to end of round.
NEXT ROUND: (From first needle) k2, p1, k1, p2, k2, p2,
k1, p1, k2, p1, k1, p2, k1, p1, k2, (from second needle)
p1, k1, p2, k1, p1, k2, p1, k1, p2, k2, p2, k1 (from third
needle) p1, k2, p1, k1, p2, k1, p1, k2, p1, k1, p2, k1, p1,
(from fourth needle) k2, p1, k1, p2, k2, p2, k1, p1, k2, p1,
k1, p2, k1, p1, k2.
Repeat the last round a further 11 times.
Change to 2.75mm double-pointed needles.
ROUND 1: (From first needle) k2, p1, k1, p2, k2, p2, k1,
p1, k2, p1, k1, p2, k1, p1, k2, (from second needle) k17,
(from third needle) k17, (from fourth needle) k2, p1, k1,
p2, k2, p2, k1, p1, k2, p1, k1, p2, k1, p1, k2.
Repeat the last round a further 4 times.
ROUND 6 (DEC ROUND): (From first needle) k1, ssk, k1,
p2, k2, p2, k1, p1, k2, p1, k1, p2, k1, p1, k2, (from second
needle) k17, (from third needle), k17, (from fourth needle)
k2, p1, k1, p2, k2, p2, k1, p1, k2, p1, k1, p2, k1, k2tog, k1.
Cont working as set, working a dec round on the foll 5th,
23rd, 28th and 48th rounds. *68 sts.*

SHAPE HEEL
NOTE: Cont to work in rows rather than rounds across the
34 sts on first and fourth needles to form heel flap. Hold
other 34 sts on second and third needles for sock upper.
NEXT ROW: (From first needle) k17, turn.
NEXT ROW: P34, turn.
ROW 1: Sl1, k33, turn.
ROW 2: Sl1, p33, turn.
Repeat these last 2 rows a further 15 times.
ROW 1: Sl1, k21, ssk, turn.
ROW 2: Sl1, p10, p2tog, turn.

KNITTING IN THE ROUND ON NEEDLES

"The beauty of knitting in the round with double-pointed needles is that you are always working a right side row. Most knitters can knit quicker than they can purl so, once you get used to handling the needles, this method is nice and quick."

STEP 1 Distribute the stitches evenly over four needles, then use the fifth empty needle to work the stitches. Mark the beginning and end of each round with a stitch marker or coloured thread.

ROW 3: Sl1, k10, ssk, turn.
ROW 4: Sl1, p10, p2tog, turn.
Rep Rows 3 and 4 a further 9 times until 12 sts rem for heel.
NEXT ROW: K12 heel sts, pick up and k 17 sts from row ends up first side of heel flap, k 34 sts held on second and third needles for upper, pick up and k 17 sts from row ends of second heel flap and then knit the first 6 heel sts again. *80 sts.*
There are now 23 sts on first needle, 17 sts on second needle, 17 sts on third needle and 23 sts on fourth needle. Cont working in rounds as folls:
ROUND 1: (From first needle) k20, k2tog, k1, (from second needle), k17, (from third needle) k17, (from fourth needle) k1, ssk, k to end of round.
ROUND 2: K to end of round.
Repeat these last 2 rounds until there are 17 sts on both the 1st and 4th needles. *68 sts.*

SHAPE FOOT
Cont to work in st st until foot measures 19cm from back of heel or 6.5cm less than required finished foot length.

SHAPE TOE
ROUND 1: K to last 3 sts on 1st needle, k2tog, k2, ssk, k to last 3 sts on 3rd needle, k2tog, k2, ssk, k to end of round.
ROUND 2: K to end of round.
Repeat the last 2 rows until 20 sts rem, ending with a Round 1. *20 sts.*
NEXT ROUND: K 5 sts on 1st needle, break off yarn leaving a long tail of approximately 30cm to sew up sock.

TO MAKE UP
Place 10 sts from second and third needles onto one needle, then place 10 sts from first and fourth needles onto another needle. Using long tail threaded through a darning needle, graft sets of stitches together as folls: Hold two needles together, parallel, with needle from which long tail comes from at back. Insert darning needle purlwise into first stitch on front needle. Pull yarn through, leaving stitch on knitting needle. Insert darning needle knitwise into first stitch on back needle. Pull yarn through, leaving stitch on knitting needle. Insert darning needle knitwise into first stitch on front needle and slip stitch off needle. Insert darning needle purlwise into next stitch on front needle, pull yarn through, leaving stitch on needle. Insert darning needle purlwise into first stitch on back needle and slip stitch off needle. Repeat until all stitches have been grafted. Weave yarn end into inside of sock. Using A, work large French knots all over foot of sock.

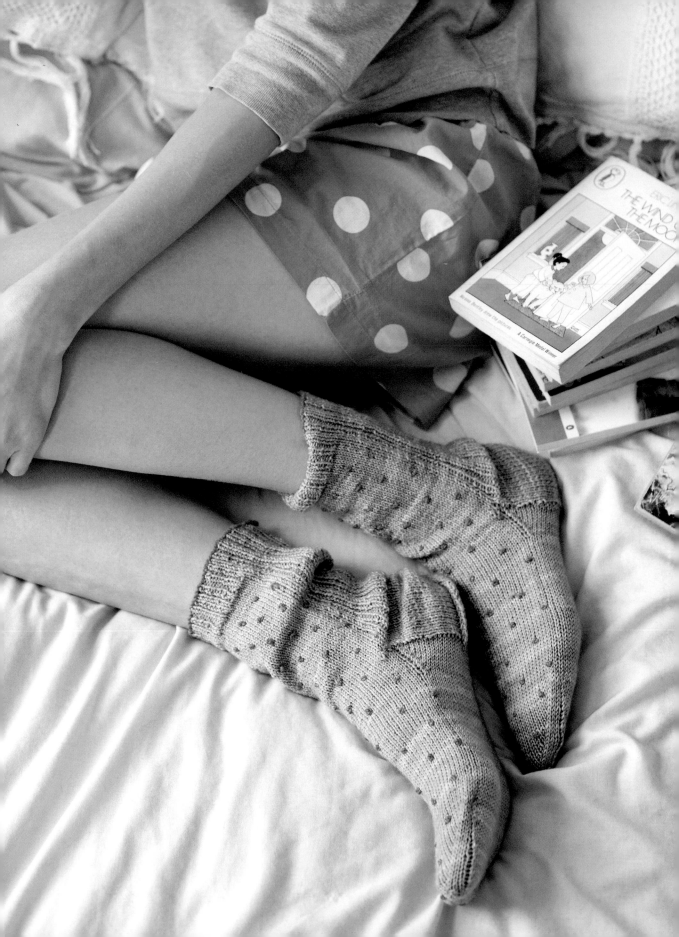

CABLED CARDIGAN
WITH SHORT SLEEVES

SIZE

UK	8	10	12	14	16
TO FIT BUST (CM)	81	86	91	97	102
TO FIT BUST (IN)	32	34	36	38	40
ACTUAL BUST (CM)	86	91	97	102	108
ACTUAL BUST (IN)	34	36	38	40	42
LENGTH (CM)	53	55	57	59	61
LENGTH (IN)	21	21½	23	23	24
SLEEVE SEAM (CM)	16	16	16	16	16
SLEEVE SEAM (IN)	6½	6½	6½	6½	6½

YARN

MC 5 (5: 6: 6: 7) x 100g hanks double-knitting weight
wool yarn, such as Juno Fibre Arts Pearl DK, in dusky
pink (Savannah)

A 1 x 50g ball double-knitting weight wool yarn, such
as Frog Tree Alpaca Sportsweight, in pink (Rose), for
buttons and edgings (optional)

Pair each of size 3.25mm and 4mm knitting needles

2.75mm, 3mm and 3.5mm crochet hooks

Cable needle

Tapestry needle

10 medium buttons

Small amount of polyester stuffing for buttons (optional)

TENSION

22 sts and 30 rows over 10cm square over stocking stitch
using 4mm needles. Adjust needle size as necessary to
obtain tension.

ABBREVIATIONS

C2B Cable two back – Slip 2 sts onto cable needle and
leave at back of work, k next st, then k 2 sts from cable
needle.

C1F slip 1 st onto cable needle and leave at front of work, k
next 2 sts, then k 1 st from cable needle.

CROSS 2 LEFT ignore first stitch, knit into back of second
stitch passing behind first stitch, knit into back of first
stitch, pass both stitches off the needle together.

CROSS 2 RIGHT ignore first stitch, purl into second stitch
passing in front of first stitch, purl into first stitch, drop
both stitches off the needle together .

See also standard abbreviations on page 7.

FANCY STRIP PATTERN
(12-ROW REPEAT WORKED OVER 6 STS)

ROWS 1, 3 AND 11: K6.

ROW 2 AND ALL EVEN-NUMBERED ROWS: P6.

ROW 5, 7 AND 9: C2B, C1F.

Repeat rows 1–12.

CROSSED STITCH PATTERN
(2-ROW REPEAT WORKED OVER 2 STS)

ROW 1: Cross 2 Left.

ROW 2: Cross 2 Right.

Repeat rows 1–2.

TO MAKE BACK

Using 4mm needles and MC, cast on 112 (118: 124: 128:
134) sts.

The Fancy Strip and Crossed Stitch patts are placed along
row with reverse stocking stitch (rev st st) at ends of row
as folls:

ROWS 1, 3 AND 11 (RS): P 3 (6: 3: 5: 8), k 0 (0: 6: 6: 6),
* [Cross 2 Left] four times, k6; rep from * 6 times,
[Cross 2 Left] four times, k 0 (0: 6: 6: 6), p 3 (6: 3: 5: 8).

ROW 2 AND ALL EVEN-NUMBERED ROWS: K 3 (6: 3: 5: 8),

p 0 (0: 6: 6: 6), * [Cross 2 Right] four times, p6; rep from * 6 times, [Cross 2 Right] four times, p 0 (0: 6: 6: 6), k 3 (6: 3: 5: 8).

ROWS 5, 7 AND 9: P 3 (6: 3: 5: 8), [C2B, C1F] 0 (0: 1: 1: 1) times * [Cross 2 Left] four times, C2B, C1F; rep from * 6 times, [Cross 2 Left] four times, [C2B, C1F] 0 (0: 1: 1: 1) times, p 3 (6: 3: 5: 8).

These 12 rows set the Fancy Strip and four sets of Crossed Stitch pattern.

Cont to work in patt as set until 24 (24: 26: 26: 28) rows have been worked.

Change to 3.25mm needles.

Cont to work in patt as set for a further 22 rows BUT work 2 rev st st, 2 crossed sts, 2 rev st st for Crossed Stitch bands.

Change to 4mm needles.

Cont to work in patt as set for a further 68 (70: 72: 74: 76) rows BUT work 3 rev st st, 1 crossed st, 3 rev st st for Crossed Stitch bands.

Cont to work in patt as set BUT cast off 6 (7: 7: 7: 8) sts at beg of next 2 rows, cast off 3 sts at beg of next 4 rows and cast off 2 sts at beg of next 2 (4: 4: 4: 4) rows.

Cont to work in patt as set but dec 1 st at beg of next 2 (–: 2: 4: 4) rows. *82 (84: 88: 90: 94) sts.*

Cont to work in patt as set without shaping for a further 20 (22: 24: 24: 28) rows, ending with a 12th (4th: 12th: 4th: 12th) row of Fancy Strip patt.

FOR 1ST SIZE ONLY
Dec 1 st at beg of next 2 rows. *80 sts.*

FOR ALL SIZES
Cast off 2 sts at beg of next 10 (12: 8: 6: 2) rows, cast off 3 sts at beg of next – (–: 4: 6: 10) rows, cast off 6 sts at beg of next 2 rows, cast off 10 sts at beg of next 2 rows.
Cast off rem 28 sts.

TO MAKE LEFT FRONT

Using 4mm needles and MC, cast on 61 (64: 67: 69: 72) sts.

The Fancy Strip and Crossed Stitch patts are placed along row with reverse stocking stitch (rev st st) at ends of row as folls:

ROWS 1, 3 AND 11 (RS): P2, * k6, [Cross 2 Left] four times; rep from * 4 times, k 0 (0: 6: 6: 6), p 3 (6: 3: 5: 8).

ROW 2 AND ALL EVEN-NUMBERED ROWS: K 3 (6: 3: 5: 8), p 0 (0: 6: 6: 6), * [Cross 2 Right] four times, p6; rep from * 3 times, k2.

ROWS 5, 7 AND 9: P2, * C2B, C1F, [Cross 2 Left] four

times; rep from * 3 times, [C2B, C1F] 0 (0: 1: 1: 1) times, p 3 (6: 3: 5: 8).

These 12 rows set the Fancy Strip and bands of four sets of Crossed Stitch patt.

Cont to work in patt as set until 24 (24: 26: 26: 28) rows have been worked.

Change to 3.25mm needles.

Cont to work in patt as set for a further 22 rows BUT work 2 rev st st, 2 crossed sts, 2 rev st st for Crossed Stitch bands.

Change to 4mm needles.

Cont to work in patt as set for a further 68 (70: 72: 74: 76) rows BUT work 3 rev st st, 1 crossed st, 3 rev st st for Crossed Stitch bands.

SHAPE ARMHOLE
Cont to work in patt as set BUT cast off 6 (7: 7: 7: 8) sts at beg of next row, cast off 3 sts at beg of 2 foll alt rows and cast off 2 sts at beg of next 1 (2: 2: 2: 2) alt rows.

Cont to work in patt as set BUT dec 1 st at beg of 1 (–: 1: 2: 2) foll alt rows. *46 (47: 49: 50: 52) sts.*

Cont to work in patt as set without shaping for a further 21 (23: 25: 25: 29) rows, ending with a 12th (4th: 12th: 4th: 12th) row of the Fancy Strip patt.

FOR 1ST SIZE ONLY
Dec 1 st at beg of next row. *45 sts.*
Cont to work in patt without shaping for 1 further row.

FOR ALL SIZES
Cast off 2 sts at beg of next and 4 (5: 3: 2: –) foll alt rows.
Cont to work in patt without shaping for 1 further row.

FOR 3RD, 4TH AND 5TH SIZES ONLY
Cast off 3 sts at beg of next row and – (–: 1: 2: 4) foll alt rows.
Cont to work in patt without shaping for 1 further row.

FOR ALL SIZES
Cast off 6 sts at beg of next row.
Cont to work in patt without shaping for 1 further row.
Cast off 10 sts at beg of next row.
Cont to work in patt without shaping for 1 further row.
Cast off rem sts.

TO MAKE RIGHT FRONT

Using 4mm needles and MC, cast on 61 (64: 67: 69: 72) sts.

Work as given for Left Front but reversing all shapings and AT THE SAME TIME make a buttonhole over Rows 5 and 6 of the third Fancy Strip repeat and every foll repeat at centre front edge until 11 (11: 12: 12: 12) buttonholes have been worked as folls:

ROW 5 (BUTTONHOLE): Patt 3 sts, cast off 4 sts in patt, patt to end.

ROW 6 (BUTTONHOLE): Patt to sts cast-off on previous row, turn, cast on 4 sts, turn, patt to end of row.

TO MAKE SLEEVES (MAKE TWO)
Using 4mm needles, cast on 92 (96: 102: 106: 110) sts.

ROW 1: K into backs of sts to end of row.

ROW 2: P to end of row.

The Fancy Strip and Crossed Stitch patterns are placed along the row with reverse stocking stitch (rev st st) at ends of row as folls:

ROWS 1, 3 AND 11 (RS): P 7 (9: 12: 14: 16), * [Cross 2 Left] four times, k6; rep from * 4 times, [Cross 2 Left] four times, p 7 (9: 12: 14: 16).

ROW 2 AND ALL EVEN-NUMBERED ROWS: K 7 (9: 12: 14: 16), * [Cross 2 Right] four times, p6; rep from * 4 times, [Cross 2 Right] four times, p 7 (9: 12: 14: 16).

ROWS 5, 7 AND 9: P 7 (9: 12: 14: 16), * [Cross 2 Left] four times, [C2B, C1F]; rep from * 4 times, [Cross 2 Left] four times, p 7 (9: 12: 14: 16).

These 12 rows set the Fancy Strip and bands of four sets of Crossed Stitch pattern.

Cont to work in patt as set until 24 rows have been worked.

Cont to work in patt as set for a further 24 rows BUT work 2 rev st st, 2 crossed sts, 2 rev st st for Crossed Stitch bands.

SHAPE SLEEVEHEAD
Cont to work in patt as set BUT work 3 rev st st, 1 crossed st, 3 rev st st for Crossed Stitch bands and AT THE SAME TIME dec 1 st at each end of every row until 28 sts rem.

Cont to work in patt without shaping for a further 28 (30: 32: 34: 36) rows.

Cast off rem sts.

TO MAKE COLLAR
Using 4mm needles and MC, cast on 112 sts.

ROWS 1, 3 AND 11 (RS): P3, * [Cross 2 Left] four times, k6; rep from * 6 times, [Cross 2 Left] four times, p3.

ROW 2 AND ALL EVEN-NUMBERED ROWS: K3, * [Cross 2 Right] four times, p6; rep from * 6 times, [Cross 2 Right] four times, p3.

ROWS 5, 7 AND 9: P3, * [Cross 2 Left] four times, C2B,

C1F; rep from * 6 times, [Cross 2 Left] four times, p3.

These 12 rows set the Fancy Strip and bands of four sets of Crossed Stitch pattern.

Cont to work in patt as set for a further 12 rows BUT work 2 rev st st, 2 crossed sts, 2 rev st st for Crossed Stitch bands.

Cont to work in patt as set for a further 12 rows BUT work 3 rev st st, 1 crossed st, 3 rev st st for Crossed Stitch bands.

Cast off.

TO MAKE UP
NOTE: The top narrow section of the sleevehead forms the shoulder.

Join the top side edges of the sleevehead to the front and back shoulder, then set in remainder of sleeve.

Sew the sleeve and side seams using mattress stitch.

Sew on the collar 2.5cm in from the front neck edge on both sides.

NOTE: This is to allow the cardigan to button up.

ADD CROCHET EDGING (OPTIONAL)
Using 2.75mm crochet hook and A, work a row of dc up Right Front edge, around Collar edge and down Left Front edge.

Work a row of dc all the way round the bottom edge of completed garment.

Work a row of dc all the way round the cast-on edge of Sleeves.

Using 3.5mm crochet hook and A, work picot edge into dc rows on Collar, Sleeves and bottom edge of completed garment as folls:

* 3 chain, 1 crochet st into next st; rep from * to end.

TO MAKE BUTTONS (OPTIONAL)
Using 3mm crochet hook and A, make 4 chain sts and slip st into a ring. Crochet in rounds until you have a disc approximately 2cm in diameter. Place a small amount of polyester toy stuffing in centre of the crocheted disc, draw the crochet up around the stuffing and fasten off.

Sew buttons onto Left Front buttonband to correspond with buttonholes on Right Front.

TARTAN SWEATER
WITH THREE-QUARTER LENGTH SLEEVES

SIZE

UK	8	10	12	14	16
TO FIT BUST (CM)	81	86	91	97	102
TO FIT BUST (IN)	32	34	36	38	40
LENGTH (CM)	47	49	51	53	55
LENGTH (IN)	18½	19	20	21	22
SLEEVE SEAM (CM)	34	35	36	37	38
SLEEVE SEAM (IN)	13½	13¾	14	14½	15

" THE TARTAN PATTERN HERE IS BUILT UP by knitting an initial Fair Isle strip sequence and then the vertical lines of colour are added by top-stitching post knitting. These vertical lines can be omitted if preferred, as the initial pattern is interesting in itself. Or you can stitch as many or as few of these verticals as you choose, but do build them up in the order suggested. The side gussets add an interest to the shape and mean that, although there are more pieces to knit, none of the tartan pieces will be too wide and so are easier to manage.**"**

YOU WILL NEED

MC 5 (5: 5: 6: 6) x 25g balls 4-ply wool yarn, such as Jamieson & Smith 2-ply Jumper Weight yarn in beige (FC45)

4-ply wool yarn, such as Jamieson's Spindrift, Rowan Pure Wool 4-ply and J.C. Rennie Unique Shetland 4-ply in the following colours:

A 3 (3: 4: 4: 4) x 25g balls in gold (Spindrift, Yellow Ochre)
B 2 (2: 2: 2: 2) x 25g balls in mid green (Spindrift, Chartreuse)
C 2 (2: 2: 2: 2) x 25g balls in brown (Spindrift, Sunrise)
D 1 (1: 1: 1: 1) x 25g ball in orange (Spindrift, Amber)
E 1 (2: 2: 2: 2) x 25g balls in mid blue (Spindrift, Teviot)
F 1 (1: 1: 1: 1) x 25g ball in pale pink (Spindrift, Oyster)
G 1 (1: 1: 1: 1) x 25g ball in dark green (Spindrift, Mermaid)
H 1 (2: 2: 2: 2) x 25g balls in deep pink (Spindrift, Lipstick)
I 2 (2: 2: 2: 2) x 50g balls in light blue (Pure Wool 4-ply, Eau de Nil)
J 1 (1: 1: 1: 1) x 50g ball in beige (Unique Shetland 4-ply, Pancake)

Pair each of 2.75mm, 3mm and 3.25mm knitting needles

TENSION

22 sts and 44 rows over 10cm square worked over moss st using 3.25mm needles and Shetland Spindrift. If you need to adjust needle size to attain this tension, then adjust needles for tartan accordingly.

ABBREVIATIONS

See the standard abbreviations on page 7.

PATTERN NOTES

Use the stranding technique, whereby the yarn not in use is carried along the wrong side of the work. If a yarn is carried for a large number of stitches, link it at intervals of a maximum of 4 stitches. Within each row, a maximum of two yarns are ever worked. The extra verticals shown on the chart are added later using duplicate stitch.

TO MAKE THE BACK

Using 3mm needles and A, cast on 133 (141: 149: 157: 165) sts.

Work in st st following Fair Isle pattern from chart, starting with Row 1, observing start point for your particular size as marked, and bringing in other colours as required and AT THE SAME TIME dec 1 st at each end of every 2nd (3rd: 3rd: 3rd: 3rd) row until there are 107 (119: 127: 135: 143) sts.

Cont to work in patt without shaping for a further 27 (22: 24: 25: 27) rows. *

Taking new sts into patt, inc 1 st at each end of every 3rd (4th: 4th: 4th: 4th) row until there are 133 (141: 149: 157: 165) sts.

Cont to work in patt without shaping until work measures 28 (29: 30: 31: 32)cm, ending with a WS row.

SHAPE ARMHOLES

Cast off 5 (7: 8: 8: 10) sts at beg next 2 rows.

Dec 1 st at each end of next 4 (3: 5: 8: 7) rows, and then at each end of 1 (2: 2: 1: 2) foll alt row(s), then each end foll 3rd (3rd: 5th: 5th: 6th) row, and then on foll 6th (5th: –: –: –) row. *109 (113: 117: 121: 125) sts.*

Work without shaping until armhole measures 18 (19: 20: 21: 22)cm, ending with a WS row.

SHAPE BACK NECK AND SHOULDERS

Work until there are 35 (37: 39: 41: 43) sts on RH needle and turn, leaving rem sts on a holder.

Work each side of neck separately.

Cast off 5 sts at beg of next row.

NEXT ROW (RS): Dec 1st at end of row.

NEXT ROW: Dec 1 st at beg of row.

NEXT ROW (RS): Cast off 8 (9: 9: 10: 11) sts at beg row and dec 1 st at end.

NEXT ROW: Dec 1 st at beg, work to end of row.

NEXT ROW: Cast off 8 (9: 10: 10: 11) sts, work to end of row.

NEXT ROW: Dec 1 st, work to end of row.

Cast off rem 9 (9: 10: 11: 11) sts.

With RS facing, rejoin yarn to rem sts, cast off centre 39 sts, work to end.

Work 1 row then complete to match first side of neck, maintaining patt and reversing all shaping.

TO MAKE THE FRONT

Work as given for Back to *. *107 (119: 127: 135: 143) sts.*

Now shape sides again, bringing new sts into patt, by inc 1 st at each end of every 3rd (4th: 4th: 4th: 4th) row until there are 121 (131: 143: 153: 163) sts.

Work 3 further rows without shaping (i.e. 1st size has inc on this last row).

DIVIDE FOR NECK

(The rate of inc of 1 st at each end of every 3rd (4th: 4th: 4th: 4th) row needs to be maintained for a while – so think about when your last inc row was and maintain this patt. These incs will now only be at side edges.)

NEXT ROW (RS FACING, IF NOT, THEN PASS STS TO OTHER NEEDLE): Work until there are 32 (36: 43: 48: 52) sts on RH needle, turn, leaving rem sts on a stitch holder. Work each side of front neck separately.

Cont side edge shaping as before, as stated, until there are 37 (41: 45: 49: 53) sts.

Cont without shaping until work measures 28 (29: 30: 31: 32)cm and matches Back to this point, ending with a WS row.

SHAPE ARMHOLE

NEXT ROW (RS): Cast off 5 (7: 8: 8: 10) sts, work to end. Work 1 row.

Dec 1 st at armhole edge on next 4 (3: 5: 8: 7) rows, 1 (2: 2: 1: 2) foll alt rows, then foll 3rd (3rd: 5th: 5th: 6th) row, and then foll 6th (5th: –: –: –) row. *25 (27: 29: 31: 33) sts.*

Cont to work in patt without shaping until armhole measures 19 (20: 21: 22 23)cm, ending with a WS row.

NEXT ROW: Cast off 8 (9: 9: 10: 11) sts at beg row. Work 1 row.

NEXT ROW: Cast off 8 (9: 10: 10: 11) sts at beg row. Work 1 row.

Cast off rem 9 (9: 10: 11: 11) sts.

With RS facing, rejoin yarn to rem sts, cast off 59 sts, work to end.

Complete to match first side of Front, maintaining patt and reversing all shaping.

TO MAKE THE SIDE PANELS (MAKE TWO)

Using 3mm needles and A, cast on 57 (67: 71: 75: 79) sts. Work as given for Back, placing patt centrally.

Shape sides by dec 1 st at each end of every 4th (6th: 6th: 6th: 6th) row, until 45 (55: 61: 65: 69) sts rem.

Work another 2 (–: 4: 4: 4) rows, ending with Row 26 (36: 34: 34: 34) of patt.

Break yarns.

Change to 2.75mm needles and MC only.

Work in single rib (k1, p1 rib), dec evenly in rib as folls: * K1, p2tog; rep from * to end (working any rem sts at end of row as single rib sts) along first of these rib rows. *30 (37: 41: 44: 46) sts.*

WORKING DUPLICATE STITCH

"Duplicate stitch, which is also known as Swiss darning, is a form of embroidery made to look like knit stitches. Using a tapestry needle threaded with coloured yarn, small areas of highlight colour can be sewn over the surface of a knitted stitch to add decorative detail without the tricky technique of knitting with multiple colours. When working duplicate stitch, do not pull the embroidered stitches too tight as the fabric will pucker."

STEP 1 Thread a tapestry needle with the highlight colour yarn. Bring the needle through from the back to the front of the fabric at the base of the stitch that is to be embroidered over.

STEP 2 Take the tapestry needle, from right to left, under the two loops of the stitch above the one being embroidered over.

STEP 3 Take the needle back through from the front to the back of the fabric at the base of the stitch where it originally came out to complete the duplicate stitch.

STEP 4 If working a horizontal row of duplicate stitches, take the tapestry needle across and bring it through the base of the next stitch to the left and continue as before.

FOR 1ST SIZE ONLY
Rib section is worked without shaping.

FOR 2ND, 3RD, 4TH AND 5TH SIZES ONLY
Cont to work decs as set of 1 st at each end of every 6th row, even within this rib, until – (33: 35: 38: 40) sts rem and then cont to work in single rib without shaping.

ALL SIZES
Work a total of 32 (26: 28: 28: 30) rib rows, from beg of rib, inc evenly as folls: * k into front and back of knit st, p1; rep from * working any remaining sts as single rib, with an additional inc st if necessary to obtain number of sts required along last rib row. *45 (49: 53: 57: 61) sts.*
Break off MC yarn, change to 3mm needles and resume patt on Row 55 (59: 59: 59: 61), ensuring patt is central. As you work, shape sides by inc 1 st at each end of every 6th (8th: 8th: 8th: 8th) row until there are 57 (67: 71: 75: 79) sts.
Cont until Side Panel measures 28 (29: 30: 31: 32)cm, up to and including last patt row worked for Back prior to armhole shaping.
Break off yarns.
Using 3.25mm needles and MC only, work from now on in moss st, using the first moss row to dec sts evenly until 39 (45: 47: 51: 53) sts rem (this means working * k1, p2tog; rep from * for most of this row).
Dec 1 st at each end of foll alt row and then every foll 3rd row until there are 3 sts.
Cont to work in moss st for a further 2 rows.
NEXT ROW: Sl1, moss st 1, psso.
Fasten off.

TO MAKE THE NECK PANELS (MAKE TWO)
Using 3.25mm needles and MC, cast on 1 st.
K into front and back of this st to make 2 sts.
Working in moss st, inc at beg of every alt row, until there are 41 sts.
Cast off in moss st.

TO MAKE THE SLEEVES (MAKE TWO)
Using 2.75mm needles and MC, cast on 49 (51: 53: 55: 57) sts.
Inc 1 st at each end of every 8th row, work in single rib (k1, p1 rib) for 18 rows.
Change to 3.25mm needles.
Work from now on in moss st, maintaining your inc patt, until there are 57 (59: 61: 63: 65) sts.
Cont to work in moss st without shaping for 3 further

rows until Sleeve measures 8cm.
Inc 1 st at each end of every 14th (13th: 12th: 11th: 10th) row until there are 73 (77: 81: 85: 91) sts.
Cont to work in moss st without shaping until Sleeve measures 34 (35: 36: 37: 38)cm, ending with a WS row.

SHAPE SLEEVEHEAD
Cast off 3 (5: 5: 5: 7) sts at beg of next 2 rows.
Dec 1 st at each end of next 3 (3: 3: 4: 4) rows, foll 2 (2: 5: 5: 7) alt rows, foll 2 (2: 1: 1: –) 3rd row(s), foll 1 (1: 1: 2: –) 4th row(s), foll 4 (4: 7: 7: 9) 5th rows, foll 1 (2: –: –: –) 4th row(s), foll 3 (3: –: 1: 1) 3rd row(s), then foll 3 (4: 4: 1: 2) alt row(s).
Dec 1 st at each end of next 4 (2: 5: 7: 6) rows.
Cast off rem 21 (21: 19: 19: 19) sts in moss st patt.

TO FINISH
Sew in any loose yarn ends.
Lightly press the tartan pattern pieces under a damp cloth.
Do not press any moss stitch or rib stitch sections.
Using duplicate stitch (see instructions given on page 129), embroider the vertical lines over the tartan pattern following the charts on pages 132 and 133. Work the centre stitch column in F (pale pink) and then work symmetrically from outwards in the foll colours: B (mid green), H (deep pink), C (brown) and G (dark green). If preferred, this additional embroidery may be omitted.
Join the shoulder seams using mattress stitch.
Set in the sleeves, matching the centre points of the sleeveheads to the shoulder seams.
Join the Side Panels to the Back at each side using mattress stitch, matching tartan patterns.
Join remaining Side Panel seams to the Front.
Join sleeve seams.
Slip stitch Neck Inserts into position, overlapping pieces right over left.
Using blanket stitch and deep pink yarn, neaten the raw edges along the back neck and down each side of the front neck as far as the Neck Inserts.
If duplicate stitch has been added, using A, embroider a line of cross stitch along the inside bottom edge of the pattern pieces to prevent curling. Repeat along back neck. If duplicate stitch has not been added, the fabric may curl at lower edge. To prevent curling, add an edging as folls: Using a 3.25mm circular needle and MC, pick up and k 253 (277: 293: 309: 325) sts evenly all round base of garment. Work in moss st for 3cm. Cast off in moss st. This adds 3cm to the length given for each size.

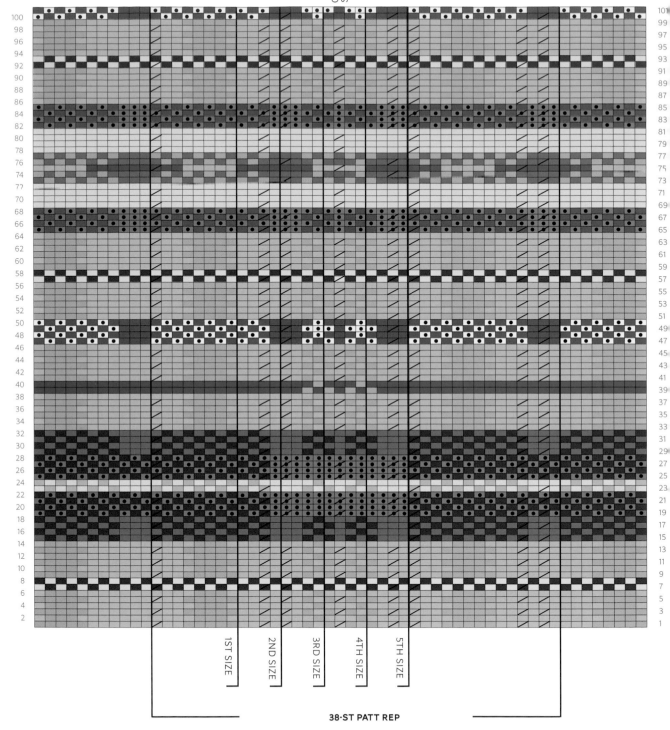

CENTRE STITCH

1ST SIZE
2ND SIZE
3RD SIZE
4TH SIZE
5TH SIZE

38-ST PATT REP

CHART NOTES
For Right Side (knit) rows, read chart from right to left and for Wrong Side (purl) rows, read chart from left to right. When starting Row 1, work from line for given size to set position of tartan pattern.

CENTRE
STITCH

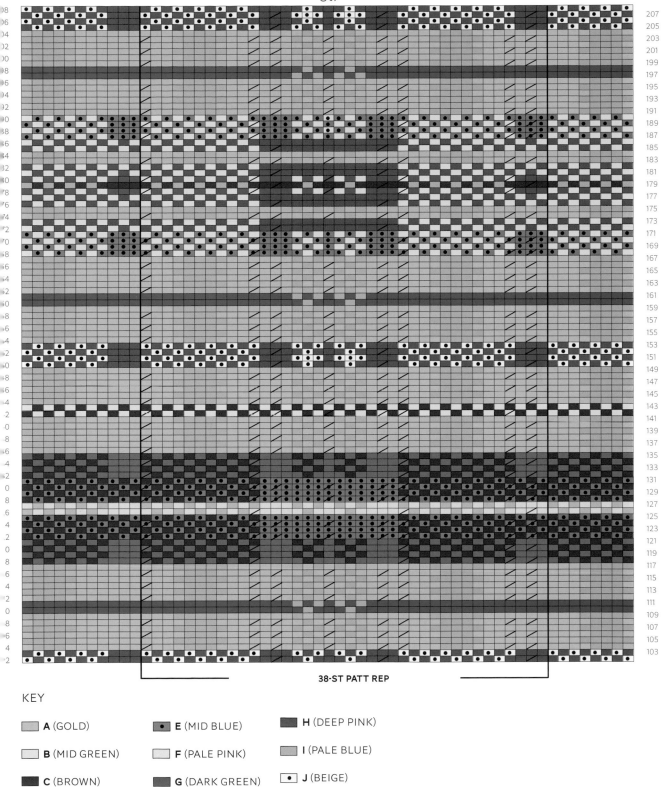

38-ST PATT REP

KEY

A (GOLD)

B (MID GREEN)

C (BROWN)

D (ORANGE)

E (MID BLUE)

F (PALE PINK)

G (DARK GREEN)

H (DEEP PINK)

I (PALE BLUE)

J (BEIGE)

TWEED CAPE

SIZE

UK	S/M	M/L
TO FIT BUST (CM)	81–91	97–102
TO FIT BUST (IN)	32–36	38–40
LOWER EDGE (CM)	157	174
LOWER EDGE (IN)	62	69
LENGTH (CM)	45.5	49
LENGTH (IN)	18	18

"**THIS CAPE IS WORKED IN SLIP STITCH,** which couldn't be easier. You simply pass the slipped stitch over from the left-hand needle to the right-hand needle and carry on knitting as normal. As you will be working with a large number of stitches, make sure your straight needles are long enough or – better still – use a circular needle with a wire, but remember you are working in rows rather than rounds."

YOU WILL NEED

A   7 (9) x 50g hanks double-knitting weight wool yarn, such as Blue Sky Alpaca Melange, in mustard (Dijon)

B   4 (6) x 100g hanks double-knitting weight mohair yarn, such as Blueberry Angora Pure Kid Mohair DK, in teal (Teal)

C   1 (1) x 50g hank double-knitting weight wool, such as Blue Sky Alpaca Sports Weight, in bright pink (Hibiscus) (optional)

Pair of long 3.25mm long knitting needles or 3.25mm circular needle, 80cm long

2 or 3 stitch holders

1 large button

TENSION

28 sts and 62 rows to 10cm square worked over slip stitch pattern on 3.25mm needles. Adjust needle size as necessary to obtain tension.

ABBREVIATIONS

See standard abbreviations on page 7.

SLIP STITCH PATTERN USED THROUGHOUT
(A 12-ROW REPEAT)

ROWS 1 AND 2: With A, k1, sl1, k4, sl1, * k2, sl1, k4, sl1; rep from * to last st, k1.
ROWS 3 AND 4: With B, k3, sl2, * k2, sl2; rep from * to last 3 sts, k3.
ROWS 5 AND 6: As Rows 1 and 2.
ROWS 7 AND 8: With B, k2, sl1, k2, sl1, * k4, sl1, k2, sl1; rep from * to last 2 sts, k2.
ROWS 9 AND 10: With A, k3, sl2, * k2, sl2; rep from * to last 3 sts, k3.
ROWS 11 AND 12: As Rows 7 and 8.

NOTE: When working the slip stitch patt, on WS rows move the yarn to the wrong side of the work when slipping a stitch purlwise to avoid strands of yarn across your work.

TO MAKE THE CAPE
(KNITTED IN ONE MAIN PIECE)
Using 3.25mm needles and B, cast on 392 (416) sts.
Work the 12-row repeat slip stitch pattern until work measures 7.5 (10)cm, ending with a WS row.

MAKE RIGHT ARMHOLE
NEXT ROW (RS): Patt 46 (54) sts, turn, leave rem unworked sts on a stitch holder.
Cont to work in patt as set for a further 24 (24)cm on these 46 (54) sts only, ending with a WS row.
Place these 46 (54) sts on another stitch holder.
With RS facing, rejoin yarn to 346 (362) sts left on stitch holder and work in patt to end of row.

MAKE LEFT ARMHOLE
NEXT ROW (WS): Patt 46 (54) sts, turn, leave rem unworked sts on a stitch holder.
Cont to work a further 24 (24)cm in patt on these 46 (54) sts only to match right side, ending with same patt row.
Place these 46 (54) sts on another stitch holder.
With WS facing, rejoin yarn to centre 300 (308) sts and work in patt to end of row.
Cont to work as folls:
ROWS 1 AND 2: Patt to end of row.
ROWS 3, 4, 5 AND 6: Patt 45 (45) sts, k2tog, patt to end of row.
ROWS 7 AND 8: Patt to end of row.
ROWS 9, 10, 11 AND 12: Patt 44 (44) sts, k2tog, patt to end of row.
Cont to work in patt but AT THE SAME TIME dec 1 st on every 3rd, 4th, 5th and 6th rows as set, reducing the

number of sts worked before each dec, until 248 (256) sts rem.
NOTE: Adjust slip stitch patt as you work to allow for decs. Work should measure 24 (24)cm to match both sides, ending with the same patt row.
Break yarn.
With RS facing, rejoin yarn to sts on stitch holder and work 1 row in patt across all sts from both stitch holders and central section.
ROW 1: Patt to end of row. *340 (364) sts.*
ROW 2 AND ALL EVEN-NUMBERED ROWS: Patt to end of row.
ROW 3: Patt 66 (66) sts, k2tog, patt to last 68 (68) sts, k2tog, patt to end of row.
ROW 5: Patt 45 (45) sts, k2tog, patt to last 47 (47) sts, k2tog, patt to end of row.
ROW 7: Patt 65 (65) sts, k2tog, patt to last 67 (67) sts, k2tog, patt to end of row.
ROW 9: Patt 44 (44) sts, k2tog, patt to last 46 (46) sts, k2tog, patt to end of row.
ROW 11: Patt 64 (64) sts, k2tog, patt to last 66 (66) sts, k2tog, patt to end of row.
ROW 12: Patt to end of row.
Rep the last 12 rows a further 3 times, reducing the number of sts worked before each dec.
ROW 1 (BUTTONHOLE): Patt 4 sts, cast off 8 sts, patt to end of row.
ROW 2 (BUTTONHOLE): Patt to last 4 sts, cast on 8 sts over those cast off in previous row, patt to end of row.
Cont to work Rows 3 to 12 of 12-row repeat patt, dec as before. *290 (316) sts.*

SHAPE NECK
NEXT ROW (RS): Cast off 24 (24) sts, work until there are 30 (30) sts in patt on needle, k2tog, patt to last 56 (56) sts, k2tog, patt to end of row.
NEXT ROW: Cast off 24 (24) sts, patt to end of row. *240 (266) sts.*

SHAPE SHOULDERS
ROW 1 (RS): Patt to end of row.
ROW 2: Patt 119 (119) sts, k2tog, patt to end of row. *239 (265) sts.*
ROW 3: K2tog, patt to last 2 sts, k2tog. *237 (263) sts.*
ROW 4: Patt 118 (118) sts, k2tog, patt to end of row. *236 (262) sts.*
ROW 5: Patt 65 (65) sts, k2tog, patt to last 67 (67) sts, k2tog, patt to end of row. *234 (260) sts.*
ROW 6: Patt 116 (116) sts, k2tog, patt to end of row. *233 (259) sts.*

ROW 7: K2tog, patt to last 2 sts, k2tog. *231 (257) sts.*
ROW 8: Patt 115 (115) sts, k2tog, patt to end of row. *230 (256) sts.*
ROW 9: Patt 64 (64) sts, k2tog, patt to last 66 (66) sts, k2tog, patt to end of row. *228 (254) sts.*
ROW 10: Patt 113 (113) sts, k2tog, patt to end of row. *227 (253) sts.*
ROW 11: K2tog, patt to last 2 sts, k2tog. *225 (251) sts.*
ROW 12: Patt 112 (112) sts, k2tog, patt to end of row. *224 (250) sts.*
ROW 13: Patt 63 (63) sts, k2tog, patt to last 65 (65) sts, k2tog, patt to end of row. *222 (248) sts.*
ROW 14: Patt 110 (110) sts, k2tog, patt to end of row. *221 (247) sts.*
ROW 15: K2tog, patt to last 2 sts, k2tog. *219 (245) sts.*
ROW 16: Patt 109 (109) sts, k2tog, patt to end of row. *218 (244) sts.*
ROW 17: Patt 62 (62) sts, k2tog, patt to last 64 (64) sts, k2tog, patt to end of row. *216 (242) sts.*
ROW 18: Patt 107 (107) sts, k2tog, patt to end of row. *215 (241) sts.*
ROW 19: K2tog, patt to last 2 sts, k2tog. *213 (239) sts.*
ROW 20: Patt 106 (106) sts, k2tog, patt to end of row. *212 (238) sts.*
ROW 21: Patt 61 (61) sts, k2tog, patt to last 63 (63) sts, k2tog, patt to end of row. *210 (236) sts.*
ROW 22: Patt 104 (104) sts, k2tog, patt to end of row. *209 (235) sts.*
ROW 23: K2tog, patt to last 2 sts, k2tog. *207 (233) sts.*
ROW 24: Patt 103 (103) sts, k2tog, patt to end of row. *206 (232) sts.*
ROW 25: Patt 60 (60) sts, k2tog, patt to last 62 (62) sts, k2tog, patt to end of row. *204 (230) sts.*
ROW 26: Patt 101 (101) sts, k2tog, patt to end of row. *203 (229) sts.*
ROW 27: K2tog, patt to last 2 sts, k2tog. *201 (227) sts.*
ROW 28: Patt 99 (99) sts, k2tog, patt to end of row. *200 (226) sts.*
ROW 29: Patt 59 (59) sts, k2tog, patt to last 61 (61) sts, k2tog, patt to end of row. *198 (224) sts.*
ROW 30: Patt to end of row.
ROW 31: K2tog, patt 79 (75) sts, cast off next 36 (44) sts, patt to last 2 sts, k2tog.
Work each side separately, beg with left shoulder.
ROW 1 (WS): Patt 58 (58) sts, k2tog, patt to end of row.
ROW 2 AND ALL EVEN-NUMBERED ROWS: Patt to end of row.
ROW 3: K2tog, patt 55 (55) sts, k2tog, patt to last 2 sts, k2tog.

ROW 5: Patt 55 (55) sts, k2tog, patt to end of row.
ROW 7: K2tog, patt 52 (52) sts, k2tog, patt to last 2 sts, k2tog.
ROW 9: Patt 52 (52) sts, k2tog, patt to end of row.
ROW 11: K2tog, patt 49 (49) sts, k2tog, patt to last 2 sts, k2tog.
ROW 13: Patt 49 (49) sts, k2tog, patt to end of row.
ROW 15: K2tog, work 46 (46) sts in patt, k2tog, patt to last 2 sts, k2tog.
ROW 17: Patt 46 (46) sts, k2tog, patt to end of row.
Cast off rem 63 (67) sts.
Rejoin yarn to right shoulder and work as given for left side, reversing all shaping.

TO MAKE UP

Weave in any loose yarn ends.
The slip stitch patt creates a textured fabric that naturally lies flat, so there is no need to press the finished piece.
To round off the otherwise quite blunt cast-off edges over the shoulders, stitch these seams from the wrong side with backstitch. Start at the neck edge and work towards the shoulder, creating a curved seam for a smooth shoulder line. Finish the seam approximately 3–4cm down from the knitting. Open out the seam on the wrong side and stitch down the seam allowance to create a mini shoulder pad.

WORK COLLAR

With RS facing and starting and finishing 5cm in from outside edges, pick up 120 (120) sts along neck edge using 3.25mm needles and B.
ROW 1 (WS): K to end of row.
ROW 2: P to end of row.
ROW 3: K3, m1, k to last 3 sts, m1, k to end.
ROW 4: P to end of row.
Rep the last 4 rows one further time.
Cont in st st without shaping for a further 4 rows.
Cast off loosely.
Turn collar over to RS of work and slip stitch cast-off edge in place to secure.

ADD SURFACE EMBROIDERY (OPTIONAL)

Using C and working in backstitch, embroider additional lines over the surface of the Cape along both vertical columns and horizontal rows of stitches to create a large simple check pattern.

TO FINISH

Sew a button securely to left front neck edge to correspond with buttonhole on right front neck edge.

YARN INFORMATION

A yarn is specified for each of the designs in this book. If you use the recommended yarn, you just need to pick your preferred shade. If you use a different yarn, compare tensions to ensure the finished results will not differ wildly. There are standard yarn weights recognised throughout the industry. Hand-knit yarns range from 2-ply laceweight through to superbulky. Within any category there is a degree of tolerance, so it is important to check the tension of each yarn against that given in a pattern. The spinner's recommended tension and needle size may vary from the pattern. If so, always go with the designer's recommendation.

ARTESANO DK 100% ALPACA
100% alpaca
100m per 50g ball
recommended tension:
22 sts and 33 rows per 10cm
on 4mm needles
www.artesanoyarns.co.uk

BC-GARN SEMILLA ORGANIC DK
100% organic wool
160m per 50g ball
recommended tension:
22 sts and 33 rows per 10cm
on 4mm needles
www.bcgarn.dk

BLUE SKY ALPACA BULKY
50% alpaca, 50% wool
41m per 100g hank
recommended tension:
8 sts per 10cm on
10mm needles
www.blueskyalpacas.com

BLUE SKY ALPACA MELANGE
100% alpaca
100m per 50g hank
recommended tension:
www.blueskyalpacas.com

BLUE SKY ALPACA SPORT WEIGHT
100% alpaca
100m per 50g hank
recommended tension:
20–24 sts per 10cm on
3.25–3.75mm needles
www.blueskyalpacas.com

BLUEBERRY ANGORA PURE KID MOHAIR DK
100% mohair
220m per 100g hank
recommended tension:
22 sts and 28 rows per 10cm
on 3.75mm needles
www.blueberryangoras.co.uk

BUFFALO GOLD LUX LACE 2-PLY YARN
45% bison down, 20% silk,
20% cashmere, 15% tencel
300m per 40g hank
recommended tension:
dependent upon project
www.buffalogold.net

DEBBIE BLISS ANGEL
76% mohair, 24% silk
200m per 25g ball
recommended tension:
18–24 sts and 23–24 rows per
10cm on 3.25–5mm needles
www.debbieblissonline.com

FROG TREE ALPACA SPORT MELANGE
100% alpaca
119m per 50g ball
recommended tension:
23–26 sts per 10cm on
2.25–3.25mm needles
www.frogtreeyarns.com

FYBERSPATES SCRUMPTIOUS LACE
45% silk, 55% merino
1000m per 100g hank
recommended tension:
25–30 sts and 37 rows per
10cm on 3mm needles
www.fyberspates.co.uk

HABU NON-TWIST COTTON BOUCLÉ LACE
100% cotton
472m per 48g hank
recommended tension:
12–16 sts per 10cm on
2–2.75mm needles
www.habutextiles.com

HOOPLA JERSEY
100% cotton jersey
100m per 500g cone
recommended tension:
dependent upon project
www.hooplayarn.com

JAMIESON'S DK
100% pure new wool
55m per 25g ball
recommended tension:
25 sts and 32 rows per 10cm
on 3.75mm needles
www.jamiesonsofshetland.co.uk

JAMIESON'S SPINDRIFT 4-PLY
100% pure new wool
105m per 25g ball
recommended tension:
30 sts and 32 rows per 10cm
on 3.25mm needles
www.jamiesonsofshetland.co.uk

J.C. RENNIE UNIQUE SHETLAND 4-PLY
100% pure new wool
215m per 50g ball
recommended tension:
28 sts and 36 rows per 10cm
on 3.25mm needles
www.knitrennie.com

JUNO FIBRE ARTS PEARL DK
40% alpaca, 40% merino,
20% silk
230m per 100g hank
recommended tension:
22 sts and 29 rows per 10cm
on 4mm needles
www.etsy.com

KOIGU PREMIUM MERIO
100% merino
160m per 50g hank
recommended tension:
28 sts and 36 rows per 10cm
on 3mm needles
www.koigu.com

LAINE ST-PIERRE WOOL
50% wool, 50% polyamide fibre
10m per card or darning wool
recommended tension:
dependent upon project
www.sajou.fr

MADELINETOSH TOSH SOCK YARN
100% superwash merino wool
361m per 100g hank
recommended tension:
26–30 sts per 10cm on
3.75mm needles
www.madelinetosh.com

MALABRIGO MERINO WORSTED
100% merino wool
192m per 100g hank
recommended tension:
18 sts per 10cm on
4.5–5.5 needles
www.malabrigoyarn.com

NATURAL DYE STUDIO ANGEL LACE 2-PLY
70% alpaca, 20% silk,
10% cashmere
800m per 100g hank
recommended tension:
1.5mm–2.5mm
www.thenaturaldyestudio.com

QUINCE & CO. PUFFIN
100% wool
102m per 100g hank
recommended tension:
10–12 sts per 10cm
www.quinceandco.com

ROWAN PURE WOOL 4-PLY
100% superwash wool
160m per 50g ball
recommended tension:
28 sts and 36 rows per 10cm
on 3.25mm needles
www.knitrowan.com

ROWAN BRITISH SHEEPS BREED BOUCLÉ
100% wool
60m per 100g ball
recommended tension:
8–9 sts and 13 rows per 10cm
on 8mm needles

MEET THE TEAM

EDITORIAL DIRECTOR: Jane O'Shea
CREATIVE DIRECTOR: Helen Lewis
COMMISSIONING EDITOR: Lisa Pendreigh
DESIGNER: Claire Peters
PRODUCTION DIRECTOR: Vincent Smith
PRODUCTION CONTROLLER: Aysun Hughes
PATTERN CHECKERS: Marilyn Wilson and Patricia Major
PHOTOGRAPHER: Laura Edwards
PHOTOGRAPHER'S ASSISTANT: Laura Wetherburn
STYLIST: Jazmine Rocks
HAIR AND MAKE-UP ARTIST: Lisa Newson
MODELS: Sam at FM Model Agency, Eva and Rose at Strike Model Management and Jo Dowbekin, and also Gavin and Kirk
HAND MODEL: Chinh Hoang

First published in 2012 by Quadrille Publishing Ltd
Alhambra House, 27–31 Charing Cross Road, London WC2H 0LS
www.quadrille.co.uk

Reprinted 2012
10 9 8 7 6 5 4 3 2

Text, projects and designs © 2012 Anna Wilkinson
Photography © 2012 Laura Edwards
Artwork, design and layout © 2012 Quadrille Publishing Ltd

British Library Cataloguing-In-Publication Data
A catalogue record for this book is available from the British Library.

ISBN 978 184949 161 7

Printed in China

Quadrille
craft

www.quadrillecraft.co.uk

If you have any comments or queries regarding the instructions in this book, please contact us at enquiries@quadrille.co.uk.

For my parents, Joanna and Martin Wilkinson.

AUTHOR'S ACKNOWLEDGEMENTS

I would like to say a very special thank you to my parents, Joanna and Martin, for their continued love, help and support; and to Richard, thank you for being so understanding and putting up with my untidiness.

I would also like to thank the following people for their brilliant knitting skills and for their help in bringing the designs in this book to life – Joanna Wilkinson, Joan Wilkinson, Leslie Wilkinson, Barbara Booker, Helen Metcalfe and Lindsay McKean. I am so grateful for all the work you have done and really appreciate the long hours you have put in to help me get everything finished in time. Also, a big thank you to Susanna Samson for being so supportive and encouraging throughout the production of this book.

Lastly, but definitely not least, I want to say a huge thank you to everyone at Quadrille Publishing, in particular Lisa and Claire, and to the fabulous, talented team I have been so lucky to work with on photoshoots. Thank you for not only making this book something that I can be incredibly proud of but also for making this process as enjoyable and fun as possible. Thank you Jazmine and Laura for your energy, creativity and persistence in making every image in this book so unique and lovely. I am so grateful for all the hard work and enthusiasm that has gone into the making this book.

PUBLISHER'S ACKNOWLEDGEMENTS

Thank you to all the owners and staff who allowed us to shoot photographs in the following locations: Boho Café in Kingston, Collector's Record Centre in Kingston, Flying Cloud Café in Teddington, A French Life in Battersea, Il Molino in Battersea and The Deli Downstairs in Victoria Park. Thanks also go to the following retailers for their generous loan of clothing: Bertie, Dune and Tabio.